Stay Young at Any Age . . .

I am well aware that no one wants to look in the mirror and see *old*. (As the Queen in *Snow White and the Seven Dwarfs* said, "I've really got to give myself a day at Elizabeth Arden.") And I am well aware that our obsession with youth is so innate in us that it cannot entirely disappear, but the point is simply to *look the best you can for any age*.

It's a little more work, of course. Who am I kidding? It's a *lot* more work, but I'm here with this book to help you get through the aging years with charm and fun and smarts and, above all, with dignity and grace.

In the pages that follow, I'm going to show you, even if this isn't your life's best time, how to have a great time anyway.

Joan Rivers

Don't Count the Candles

the Candles

Just Keep the Fire Lit!

JOAN RIVERS

HarperTorch

An Imprint of HarperCollins*Publishers*

HARPERTORCH
An Imprint of HarperCollins*Publishers*
10 East 53rd Street
New York, New York 10022-5299

First HarperTorch paperback printing: May 2000
First HarperCollins hardcover printing: April 1999

HarperCollins®, HarperTorch™, and ❦™ are trademarks of HarperCollins Publishers Inc.
Avon Trademark Reg. U.S. Pat. Off. and in Other Countries, Marca Registrada, Hecho en U.S.A.

Printed in the United States of America

Visit HarperTorch on the World Wide Web at www.harpercollins.com

❖ 10 9 8 7 6 5 4 3 2 1

TO ALL THE INNOVATIVE
PLASTIC SURGEONS OF TOMORROW:
HURRY!!!

CONTENTS

One: Fine If You're Wine   1

Two: Peter Stuyvesant and I Went Dutch   9

Three: Dress Halston, Not Halloween   33

Four: Early Plastic Isn't Chic   63

Five: Climb Every Staircase   81

Six: Some People Will Swallow Anything   105

Seven: A Roll in the Hay Keeps
     the Doctor Away   129

Eight: No Fool's Gold for
     Your Golden Years   161

Nine: The Kindest Cut   187

Ten: The Luckier You Get   213

Don't Count
the Candles

ONE

Fine If You're Wine

Let me say straight off: *Aging sucks*. Put more elegantly, it's lousy. Nobody wants to get older. Nobody wants to lift her arm and see crepe paper, but there it is. I don't care how young you are: You can't say it doesn't hurt when you get into a bathing suit and don't look as good as you did ten years ago, or even five.

People who tell you that age is wonderful are lying. We've all heard this whopper: "You're not getting older, you're getting better."

Really? Is that a medical diagnosis? Then

you had better get a second opinion because I can't find my glasses to read how good I've become.

In the middle of the nineteenth century, when liposuction was still a dream and Esoterica was a young lady's name and almost no one went to Fort Lauderdale, an Englishman named Robert Browning wrote:

> **Grow old along with me.**
> **The best is yet to be.**

Clearly, this man was a minor poet. Or else, when he wrote those lines, he was twelve.

Getting older happens to be a particularly foolish direction to go in America, where almost everyone is obsessed with age, where numbers are always and pointlessly attached to every name that's published in a newspaper or magazine:

Joe Creamer, 43, and his daughter Tiffany-Ann, 9, were merrily chasing a bunny, 2, when Tiffany-Ann tripped on the root of a tree, 106.

James Thurber, the great humorist, had the right idea when he said, "The trouble with us is that we number everything. I think we deserve to have more than fourteen years between the ages of twenty-six and forty."

Any woman who says "I'm happy to be 106" is also not embracing the truth. She wishes to hell she were still forty-one. Old age is not the golden one. You're not automatically wiser. You're not automatically smarter. All you are is automatically less of a sex symbol. You might even be one of those gray people to whom nobody gravitates or talks at a party. It's awful to walk into a crowded room and be the oldest person there. You find that people are looking right through you. You've become invisible.

As British writer Anthony Powell said, "Growing old is like being increasingly penalized for a crime you haven't committed."

However, as fervently as we wish that time didn't fly but just sat in the terminal, everyone does keep getting older. Even the baby boomers. No, *especially* the baby boomers. I am always amused when a newspaper or magazine refers to an older man or woman as "an aging tax evader" or "an aging sadomasochist." Is there anyone postpartum who could be described as *younging*?

We are so idiotically hung up on age that Isabella Rossellini, one of the most ethereally beautiful women in our solar system, was fired as the face that promoted a major cosmetics company by some mentally challenged executives who felt that she had been too long out of the womb. She was forty-two years old.

"You represent the reality of beauty," they said to Isabella, "and we're selling the fantasy of it. And the fantasy is young."

One of these days, Estée Lauder may run an ad showing the shade that looks best with diapers—and I don't mean Depends.

Television's Joan Lunden, no Wicked Witch of the West, was dumped by *Good Morning America* two years ago because she was a gorgeous woman of forty instead of someone in a training bra. That's right: dumped by *Good Morning America,* the place where people are supposed to wake up and smell the coffee, where at least one producer should have been aware of the great truth that fifty is now what thirty-five used to be.

However, even though people are now living longer than ever, even though the average American life span is now seventy-six, even though 33 million people in this country are now over sixty-five, America still seems to feel that kids " Я " us. The startling truth is that, by the year 2000, more than 75 million Americans will be over fifty. Every ten seconds in America, someone turns fifty, and too many of these people think it is time to call Dr. Kevorkian (the only doctor who still makes house calls).

Okay, so despite the demographics, aging stinks. But the only way to avoid it is for your life to end now, which is an even less appealing option. Maurice Chevalier may or may not have been the first to say, "Old age isn't so bad when you consider the alternative."

Better, I say, to take stock of where you are chronologically, to realize all the baggage that comes with aging, and then not to accept it. Yes, refuse to pay the COD. I believe in fighting aging all the way, but fighting it constructively and intelligently. Doing what we *can* do to look and feel the best that we *can* look and feel. Being the best that we can possibly be.

Yes, in spite of the inevitability of aging, you *can* remake yourself and recharge your life by working on your diet, your wardrobe, your makeup, your home, your career, your volunteering, your sex (which shouldn't feel like volunteering), and, most important, your *attitude:* your constant desire to stay mentally and physically active in the mainstream of life. If you are thinking of moving to Florida to just sit in the sun while comparing bond prices, bypass stories, and beautiful grandchildren, this book is not for you. It is for people who think that the only point in living is staying alive in what Teddy Roosevelt called "the arena."

I am well aware that no one wants to look in the mirror and see *old*. (As the Queen in *Snow White and the Seven Dwarfs* said, "I've really got to give myself a day at Elizabeth Arden.") And I am well aware that our obsession with youth is so innate in us that it cannot entirely disappear, but the point is simply to *look the best you can for your age.*

It's a little more work, of course. Who am I kidding? It's a *lot* more work, but I'm here with this book to help you get through the aging years with charm and fun and smarts and, above all, with dignity and grace.

In the pages that follow, I'm going to show you, no matter what your age, how to cut the losses that the years try to thrust on you. And I'm going to show you, even if this isn't your life's best time, how to have a great time anyway.

How to Fool Yourself into Feeling Younger

- When you go to restaurants, always check a coat and a skateboard.

- Never visit anyone in a place called Sun City or Leisure *anything*.

- Ask the Motor Vehicle Bureau if, for an extra five dollars, you can retouch your driver's license photo.

- When you speak, say "like" every fifth word. And "whatever" every third.

- Wear a baseball cap backward. Of course, to the kids "backward" is the peak to the front. *You* figure it out.

TWO

Peter Stuyvesant and I Went Dutch

Before we start looking for what you may have lost, let's make sure that you should be reading this book and not *The Puff Daddy Story*. How do you know if you're old? Answer these questions, none of which comes from the examination for Mensa.

Lately, have you been finding yourself suddenly aware of being the oldest person in the room? In the state? All right, you don't feel quite *that* old, but do you feel as though you *look* it? Do you feel they are tearing down buildings that are younger than you?

No, I am not talking about the Medicare

years. Unfortunately, the perception of being a senior citizen in a junior world takes place long before sixty-five. Let's continue the quiz.

If you happen to pick up a copy of *Seventeen* in the beauty parlor, do you wonder why it is written in a foreign language?

And there are other dismaying moments of truth. Did your daughter just try on one of your dresses and make you suddenly think: *That's the way it's supposed to look.*

Are you nostalgic for the Halloween of Margaret O'Brien in *Meet Me in St. Louis*? Are you nostalgic for someone who knows who Margaret O'Brien is? Or *Pat* O'Brien— the actor, that is. Most people today who watch sportscaster Pat O'Brien don't know the Pat O'Brien who played Knute Rockne in a film. Of course, these people would also think that Knute Rockne made chairs for IKEA.

In the department of memories, are you the only one in your crowd who knows all the words of "Besame Mucho"? Do some of your friends think that Besame Mucho is a Mexican perfume?

Are you afraid to mention Paul McCartney because the person to whom you mention him won't think of the Beatles or even Wings but instead might say, "Paul McCartney? Isn't he Stella McCartney's father or something?" And if you mention the Ink Spots, do people around you think you're talking about a Rorschach test?

If your answers to all these questions are *no,* stop reading and go do your homework. However, if all your answers are *yes,* then you are ready for this book, whether you're thirty-five, forty, fifty-five, or seventy-five. You can be ready without being old enough to have been alive when tennis balls were white.

A sixty-six-year-old friend of mine, both of whose parents had died in their fifties, recently told me, "At my age, I should be dead."

I almost granted his wish right then because he was stupidly imposing a limit on himself instead of going for the moon. *He* needs this book.

So does another friend, a woman in her forties. She's crazed these days, depressed at the thought of turning fifty in a few years. And she's sobbing that it's all over: Nobody's looking at her and she can't find a man. Mind you, she's attractive, smart, and successful, but now she's letting herself go, withdrawing socially, and spoiling what could be a great time in her life.

Another person who needs this book is even younger. I saw her at an art opening on Madison Avenue. She was standing there and looking glorious, having just come from a luncheon at one of those Madison Avenue restaurants where you can't hear a thing. Couldn't have been a day over thirty-four. And then I heard her say to the young woman she was with, "I feel rotten. I feel so *old*."

I wanted to slam her against the wall. How could she not appreciate where she is now? I wanted to shake her and shout, "Idiot, don't you know that in ten years you'll look back on today and go, 'That age was great'? So why not enjoy it *now*?"

Then it hit me, of course: At *every* age, women—and most men too—have this terrible problem with growing older.

I'm thinking of Gene Hackman, for one, who has confessed that "it really costs me a lot emotionally to watch myself on-screen. I feel as though I'm quite young, and then I look at this old man with the baggy chins and the tired eyes and the receding hairline and all that."

Gene's angst is like that of Jason Robards, who at seventy-five said, "When I look in the mirror, I see an old man I didn't know was there."

Aging has given even a relative tadpole like Matt Dillon pause. "Thirty was so strange to me," he said as he left his twenties. "I have to come to terms with the fact that I am now a walking and talking adult!"

Eddie Murphy also gets edgy when he contemplates the passing of time. He's afraid that "in twenty years, I'll be looked at like Bob Hope. Doing those President jokes and golf shit. It scares me."

However, *nothing* about the accumulation of years seems to scare Farrah Fawcett. When Farrah turned a dishy fifty, she made an erotic video called *All of Me,* which celebrated, among other things, her body's defiance of gravity. On turning fifty, Gloria Steinem had said, "This is what fifty looks like." But on turning fifty, Farrah said, "This is what thirty looks like."

I must admit, of course, that her video was remarkable. If *I* had made an erotic video at fifty, it would have been called *The Gall of Me*. Or, were I not such a devotee of plastic surgery, it just as fittingly could have been called *The Fall of Me*.

As it is, I try to catch whatever it is that's even about to fall, including my face, which I've had revised from time to time. In fact, Darwin would be happy to know that my face is in a constant state of evolution.

It is often said that at fifty people have the face they deserve. Well, I deserve a different face, and you probably feel that you do too. No, not different: the same one, but made more presentable.

I know: Beauty is only skin deep. I agree with that timeless truth. However, how deep do you want it to be? Do you want a beautiful spleen?

"Do I look like a woman my age?" I once asked a friend.

"You look more like a man your age," she sweetly replied.

I know I'll never be arm candy again (in fact, I never had a first time as that particular confection), and I know I'll never be a trophy wife. But I keep trying. I know I'll never look twenty again (except in dog years), but I do want to look the best I can at every age. I'm going to hold back the inevitable for as long as possible, to keep ticket sellers from asking me, "Would you like the senior discount?" I don't want someone greeting me with the secret handshake of the AARP.

I'm going to fight old age every way I can. I'll fight with every illegal trick I know, every dishonest blow I can land. And when I eventually do die, I plan to be buried with my plastic surgeon. If you like this plan, then join me: Let's gather our forces and strike out against old age by starting with the firm belief that old age is always ten years more than we are.

And so, when we're a middle-aged ninety

(because old people are a hundred), we'll be the age P. G. Wodehouse was when he wrote his eighty-fifth book about Jeeves. We'll be ten years younger than Grandma Moses was when she painted her best primitives. And we'll be 810 years younger than Methuselah, who must have had a prostate to write home about.

A legendary horse trainer, Fred Hooper, turned one hundred last year. His horse won the Kentucky Derby in 1943, and he is still the active director of a horse farm in Florida. When asked to tell how he had managed to reach one hundred, Fred replied:

"Hard work and always look ahead. I never look back."

In short, he has remained in Teddy Roosevelt's arena, where he doesn't pause to reminisce about the midlife crisis he might have had at fifty.

Are you afraid of what you consider the trappings of age? For example, are you afraid that bifocals will make you look old? Then consider that the man who invented bifocals, Benjamin Franklin, was taking women to bed at eighty, and none of them looked at his bifocals and told him to go fly a kite.

Fred Hooper and Benjamin Franklin never feared change, and going along with change is a major factor in aging gracefully.

Change, of course, can be scary. It is fear of change that makes many older people look backward instead of ahead. And so you've got to try to make a continuous effort in dress, hair, makeup, attitude—in all the essential parts of your life—to move yourself out of the past and into the present.

Memories, of course, crowd the minds of all of us at any age. However, inflict them selectively on your friends and your kids.

"That's where the Astor Hotel used to be," I told my daughter Melissa one day while we were walking through Times Square. "And the Paramount Theatre was over there and the Capitol and the Roxy up there."

Her eyes began to glaze over, but not from nostalgia: She just passionately didn't care about my medieval days in New York. She was probably afraid that I would next be telling her where I used to meet Peter

Stuyvesant for lunch. (It was on Eighth Street and Seventh Avenue, in a darling little tavern called The Dutch Treat. Peter was a gentleman and never went Dutch treat. He always let me pay for him.)

Seven years after Leonard Bernstein died, one of his daughters decided to sell several of his possessions at auction, including his piano.

"It was wrenching," she said. "However, preserving everything the way it was keeps you stalled in the past."

She wisely knew that everyone must live in the now. It is one of the basic ways to get through aging.

Live in the now, appreciate the now, enjoy the now, be involved in the now, and make sure you are included in the now. Update your ideas, your conversation, your reading list, your home, your gadgets, your politics, your wardrobe. Keep active, keep moving forward, keep looking good. Work hard on your body, your face, your job, and your mind. My mother always believed that it's not how old you are but how you are old.

Face it: Okay, you're no longer a cupcake. People will no longer fawn all over you just for your physical presence. So, when you go to a dinner party, make sure that you'll add something. I try to always have at least three good stories to tell. And you'd better make sure that you've read the newspaper, some good books, and a few magazines, and that you've seen the hot new movie and the latest hit show. Be current. Have opinions. Know and enjoy the now.

And if you're intimate with the buzz, if you're tapped into what's going on and know what's being talked about, then you'll be able to chime in, to contribute. And guess what: You'll end up having a great time.

I can't stress this enough: You've got to keep totally current. You've got to keep up-to-date in every part of the life that keeps whirling by at a dizzying pace. This is the world where the turnover of celebrities is so fast that a teenager I know heard a song from 1994 and said, "Oh, a golden oldie."

So that you won't be a golden oldie, get a personal computer and learn how to use it;

get a fax machine, so that you can fax to high-powered friends, even if you have nothing to say; and get a cell phone, so you can join all the people who are driving in the wrong lane because they are checking on a child, a stock, or when the new drapes are coming.

Yes, modern life is challenging, but it's a challenge you have to accept, no matter how dismaying it may be.

In a movie theater a few weeks ago, I had abandoned myself to a tale of eighteenth-century France when I suddenly heard a beep, beep, beep.

"Marie Antoinette has a beeper?" I asked my friend Orin.

"No, that's coming from the audience," he replied. "It's either a doctor or a teenager."

"Why does a teenager need a beeper?"

"To be reachable at the mall, of course."

The alternative to staying current is to stay stuck in the past, where you wore pointy bras that looked like pink armor and where you always went to the ladies' room with a friend for tandem toilet time and where you had all those dates with boys your mother admired who grew up to be the dermatologists and insider traders.

It is so important to me to be thoroughly in step with modern life. Maybe things are going too fast, but since we can't stop them, we simply must accept them.

Whenever I hear someone proudly say, "I don't have a computer or fax or VCR," I want to reply, "Elvis is dead and you'd better check your pulse too."

A few months ago, a friend of mine learned the absolute necessity of staying current. Afraid of computers, she had actually been using a Smith-Corona manual typewriter, which was on its way to being a collector's item because the Smith-Corona manual has gone the way of *Tyrannosaurus rex*. And then one day, after going from one office supply store to another, my friend was dismayed to discover that she couldn't find a new ribbon.

"It was a poignant attempt to recapture the past," she told me. "Buying a ribbon for a manual typewriter today makes as much sense as shopping for a buggy whip."

She even tried a Kmart, where she said to a teenage clerk, "I'd like a manual typewriter ribbon, please."

"A manual? A ribbon?" said the clerk, seeming to feel that my friend was requesting a guide to hairstyles.

"Yes, for a manual typewriter," said my friend.

"Mac or IBM?"

And my friend sighed and said, "Windows 54."

Before my own great leap into modern life, I had a similar moment of truth when I went into a music store and tried to buy a new needle for my stereo. Those were the days when a CD was something I banked, not played.

"I would like a new needle," I said to a young female clerk.

No, that's old-fashioned too: Clerks today are called "associates." When you hear the store's manager say on the speaker system, "Will an associate please come to aisle two," you probably think that the manager needs a lawyer.

At any rate, this young associate looked at me and helpfully said, "You would like a what?"

"A needle," I said.

"Hypodermic or sewing? Anyway, I don't think we carry either one."

"Oh, of course," I said. "You call it a stylus."

"A what?" she brightly said.

"A stylus."

"Well, what style do you want? Rock? Broadway? Country and Western?"

Meanwhile, back in the here and now, the trick is to know as much of the present as you do of the past and not to look back. Looking back is bad for your mental health and even worse for your social life. Remember what looking back did to Lot's wife. And she'd been trying to stay on a low-salt diet.

And, for God's sake, never tell anyone that things were better in the good old days! Wasn't it merry when there was no penicillin? Wasn't it a lark to get polio? Can we ever recapture the innocent delight of diphtheria?

Remember the names of your children, of course, and listen to some of their music, but try never to be seen with them in public because children date you even more than reminiscing about Mamie Eisenhower.

No matter how hard we try, we can never fool children. Poor little things, they tend to tell the truth. A friend of mine had a mother who fought fiercely against age and thought she was winning: According to her scorecard, she looked half her age.

And then one day at a luncheon, she was on her way to a ladies' room when she met a girl of about six, who said, "Oh, I know you."

"Yes, who am I?" said my friend's mother.

"You're Amy's grandmother."

And the woman suddenly realized how badly she had been keeping score: that, no matter how she tried, she did look like somebody's grandmother. At that luncheon, she had considerably more wine than she had planned to drink.

French actor Gerard Depardieu once said, "At twenty you have many desires that hide the truth, but beyond forty there are only real and fragile truths—your abilities and your failings." It's the old paradox: We have to accept who we are while we fight it all the way. There's a new generation every twenty years. Or is it five? Either way, you can be an honorary part of it if you stay current and active.

So join a gym and take a pottery class and learn how to use a wok and go on the Internet. Take lessons in needlepoint or golf. You don't have to be good at it. I play golf as if I'm beating a rug, but I do it. Start listening to birds at dawn and to Bach at dusk. Start running a mile a couple of times a week. Don't worry about your speed; I do a twenty-six-minute mile, which would be impressive in a track meet at a rest home; but the important thing is I don't take a cab around the track.

You could also learn poker and have the boys in on a Friday night. If your body's in shape—and it should be—make it strip poker. Also join a reading club or sing in a glee club or raise bees. So what if you get stung. The welts will give you cocktail party talk and you'll be the center of attention, as you were at a weltless twenty.

I've left out dozens of activities that can fill you with the best kind of reward—nonfinancial—from ice skating to ceramics. In fact, try everything in life except incest and folk dancing, for one of the great benefits of being older (whatever age that is) is that you can do anything that isn't a felony and know it's all right, as long as it's current.

I'm not telling you that staying current isn't work because it is, but the alternative is to buy a nice bathrobe and make reservations at the Home. It's very easy not to get off the couch and do exhausting workouts, particularly if the woman at the next Nautilus machine is nineteen years old and makes you want to drop a barbell on her.

And it's easy not to get off the couch and go out to see that new Renoir exhibition, but you've got to do it.

So do as I say, do as I do, and you not only will change your life but will change the way you are thought of: People will know that you are still productive, still sexy, still sought-after in company. You've got to work hard, however, to make this perception happen.

Think of yourself as a bumblebee, for the bumblebee has achieved a magnificent triumph over impossible odds: According to the law of aerodynamics, the ratio of its body weight to its wingspan should render it unable to fly. But what a splendid scofflaw the bumblebee is! And what a splendid, sought-after, sexy scofflaw you can be too.

In a recent film called *Twilight,* Susan Sarandon and Paul Newman make love one night, with no EMS worker beside the bed. And at the end of the film, when Newman and Stockard Channing walk off for what will be many more nights of love, the coupling seems like two lively lovers, not seniors using an escort service.

There are scientists who now believe that the natural human life span is 120 years. In other words, your life span may top your IQ.

And here's the latest news about IQ: Contrary to popular belief, it does not decrease with age. So if your sister-in-law was a moron at twenty, she will still be a moron at seventy-five, rather than having sunk to idiot.

"The brain does not necessarily deteriorate

as we age," says Dr. Richard M. Restak, author of *The Brain and the Mind*. "It's also a myth that we suffer a significant loss of nerve cells in the brain as we age; in fact, we can actually expand the connections between neurons if we continue to be intellectually stimulated and curious."

A nice example of such expansions was Oliver Wendell Holmes, who began reading Plato at age ninety-two. Why did he do this instead of playing crazy eights? Was it because he couldn't remember where he had put the cards? No!

"To improve my mind," he said.

To show you how far mankind has come, in spite of *The Jerry Springer Show,* Holmes said a hundred years ago that old age started at forty-six. And yet, when Holmes was twice that age, he was acting young.

Eubie Blake, the great songwriter and pianist, enjoyed a hundred years of mental stimulation, during which he wrote "I'm Just Wild About Harry" and "Memories of You." When he reached ninety-eight, he said, "If I'd known I was going to live this long, I would have taken better care of myself."

So maybe he couldn't do much at the gym, but the important thing is that he kept exercising his best muscle: his brain.

I'll talk a lot more about exercising the brain in the pages to come—if I remember. (Novelist Rita Mae Brown, incidentally, believes that the true function of age is memory, and that's why she says, "I'm recording as fast as I can.") But I'm not worried that my forgetfulness will make me seem old because I know that everyone forgets at every age. For example, I have never been able to remember names, and neither could a certain notable athlete in his prime named Babe Ruth. He called every one of his Yankee teammates "kid."

Well, kid, because of wondrous advances in medicine, the downside of aging is no longer so steep: People are staying physically and mentally fit into their eighties and even their nineties: The last New York City Marathon had one runner of eighty-seven and one of ninety-one.

And in Santa Rosa, California—you may not believe this—there is a hockey league for men over seventy-five that has been organized by Snoopy's creator, Charles Schulz, a man known as "Sparky" by the skating seniors who try to flatten him on the ice. In the fight against aging, the puck stops there.

Never forget that we now have the power to make our chronological age irrelevant, unless we want the senior discount. All right, so you remember what Burma Shave signs were; but you now know that the signs today would have to say Myanmar Shave.

How to Fool Yourself into Feeling Younger
(In case the first list doesn't work.)

- At parties, never use your dentures as castanets.

- Never admit knowing anything that happened before 1945. If someone mentions World War II, reply, "World War II . . . World War II . . . We won that one, right?"

- If you want to reminisce, don't make the recollection yours. Instead say, "While passing a retirement village, I heard . . . "

- Avoid admitting that at the Last Supper, you were at the next table.

THREE

Dress Halston, Not Halloween

"There is a noticeable blurring," says Anne Marshall of the consulting firm Woman Trend. She's not talking about your vision or your makeup. She is saying, "Young people today have many of the values usually associated with older ones and older people are acting younger."

This is absolutely true of fashion. The point is that, no matter what your age, there are no rules anymore—except one: Be aware of how you look. Your clothes make a statement, and yours shouldn't be: "I look ludicrous." Instead, the statement should be: "I am not sixteen, but I am also not surrendering to age."

If you've still got the great legs, show the great legs—but know where the short skirt should stop. If you've still got the perky breasts, show the perky breasts—but know how much décolletage is too décolleté. And if you've still got the fabulous body, show the fabulous body—but know when the clinging matte jersey is clinging to the wrong parts.

One day last year, after one of the talks I've been giving to women all around America about taking control of and enriching their lives, two women in their seventies came up to me. One was dressed wonderfully, but the other looked like the poster girl for National Nursing Home Month. And I wanted to ask her:

When did you give up? And why? When did you decide it was all over and you would start modeling for a catalogue called Queen Victoria's Secret?

Sad to say, I can name a lot of women in that category, people who have caved in to age and given up trying to dress to please the eye.

In Ecclesiastes, it is written: "For everything there is a season." Ecclesiastes isn't referring to the fall season or the new line from Paris. However, in the seasons of your life, when you're playing the back nine, there's no reason you shouldn't look as chic as the Popsicle who is just teeing off. And you *can* look that way if you make smart choices.

In clothes (in hair and makeup as well; I'll get to them shortly), indeed in the whole package that makes you distinctly *you, sensible* is usually the wisest choice. And sensible means your entire package should fit into a complete whole.

In other words, don't end up making a spectacle of yourself. We all know the lady of fifty who's decided she is really twenty-two because she's reed-thin and still what you'd call built. So she puts on the Yves Saint Laurent cat suit and the crotch-high swashbucklers and struts down the street wiggling her tight little tush and looking hot hot hot. And the guys behind her are giving wolf whistles—until she turns around to thank them. And then they see the lines and bags and they cry, "Oh my God, it's Margot from Shangri-la!"

In short: Before you put on the Spandex, make sure that your *face* is still young enough to match it.

It happens in every neighborhood. On my block in Manhattan one day, I found myself walking behind a woman in a miniskirt, yellow gloves, and leopard-print tights.

A cool young chick, I thought.

And then this chick turned around and I saw the face of a hen in her fifties, wattles and all! From the front, she didn't look cool, she looked like a fool. Her tights were sporting the wrong animal: It should have been a jackass.

The better way to go at this time in your life is to make a friend of your mirror. Confer with it daily; trust what it has to say. Put on that sexy, splashy Versace, the one you wore five years ago that stirred up testosterone all over town. Then consult your friend, the mirror. Take a long, critical look and believe what you see. What would you say if you went to a party and that lady in the mirror walked in and she wasn't you? Would you say, "Good God, she looks amazing"? Or would you say, "Does she think it's Halloween?"

Check yourself out from every angle, then check again and again. After one last check, if you can honestly say you look great, then God bless you, *wear* the hot dress and see how many men you can arouse.

"But what if I look only lukewarm?" you ask.

Then, hard as it is, you've got to accept that it's time to change your look a little. You've got to realize that the time has come when there are certain changes you can't do anything about and you have to adapt.

The morning after the night before, I took a look at the tape of my performance at last year's Emmys. Well, that's the last time I'll ever wear a dress without sleeves—and I work hard on my arms. The smart women on the show were ones like Mary Tyler Moore, who was in see-through Vera Wang, but she was *covered*. No flesh dangling from her arms and wafting in the wind like pink sails. I, however, felt slightly stuck in time.

If you look around, you'll see many people who are stuck where they looked best.

I can remember the days when Elizabeth Taylor looked *beyond* sensational. It was when she was with George Hamilton, who *still* looks sensational. I saw them at Spago one night and she looked the way a movie star *should* look, the way Sophia Loren still looks when she walks into a room. (Sophia Loren doesn't go out unless she looks good.)

I myself never go out without thinking: *How do I look if I happen to bump into David Feidelson?* He was the boy who was mean to me in the ninth grade. You think I don't work on my memory?

Despite all your hard work, however, there are still times when reality comes and smacks you in the face. You have to know when the little bag is too little or the heel is too high. You have to recognize your trouble spots. Mine is heels. I have thirty-six pairs of high-heeled Manolo Blahniks in my closet. I put them on now and look like an old lady in stilts. I'm starting to switch—sob!—to medium.

Many people who should know better, don't. For example, the editor-in-chief of one of our top fashion magazines still wears tank tops. Although she's only forty-two, she has arms that are spread too much for a spread in her own magazine. She thinks she looks chic, and no one dares tell her the truth.

And so, always look current, but current for *your* age.

"But I looked really good in this outfit in 1993," you're saying.

Fine. The next time it's 1993, you can wear it again. Your wardrobe should never be a historical review.

A good way to know if you are being truly current in your dress but not stupidly faddy is to look at magazines. Not *Popular Mechanics* and not *Seventeen* or *Marie Claire,* but *Harper's Bazaar* and *Vogue.* Your goal is to look young but appropriate, so flip through the pages and pick the current look that's right for you. There's always something in every fashion that you can wear to look "with it" at your time of life.

There is nothing wrong, for example, with

wearing a sweater set with the outer sweater tied around your neck. But it should be today's sweater, not some relic from your first sock hop.

Speaking of relics, there are few things worse than going somewhere hip and realizing that the man you're with is the only man in a tie and jacket, and you're the only woman wearing a skirt. At that point, however, you've got to say, "Okay, this is where we are in life: These are the choices we've made."

One of my own choices is to dress up for the theater. I don't like going to the theater in sneakers and a sweatshirt from Kentucky Fried Chicken. There are other ways to decorate the body—and I'm not talking about tattoos.

One good way to decorate your body is to adopt a signature, something that will make you look distinctive and different as well as current. If I could, I would always wear a gardenia. Not only does a gardenia look elegant, but its scent gives both me and the people who meet me a sweet aroma.

I doubt that any living creature except her cats has seen Carrie Donovan, the great fashion icon in TV ads, without her huge black-rim glasses. She very well could look like hell behind that facade, but no one would notice because all we ever see are the glasses that give her fantastic flair.

And how about fashion doyenne Diana Vreeland's rouged ears and sleeked-back pitch black hair? So striking you hardly noticed that her shoes with their polished soles looked as though she made them herself.

Vincent Price told me about a lady who always wore a diamond bracelet even when swimming. It had been her mother's, and she never took it off. How truly sparkling was the water she swam through.

And, of course, there was Jackie Kennedy in her unforgettable pillbox hats.

Signature is style and style is an elegant thing to have. However, make sure it's your own and not borrowed from Aunt Rose. You do not want to look secondhand.

Moreover, do not be influenced by the style

of celebrities. On her television show, *Veronica's Closet,* Kirstie Alley has worn old Chinese pajamas to her office. Well, Kirstie Alley can carry that off, but *you and I* couldn't wear old Chinese pajamas to the office, even if we worked a night shift in Shanghai.

Every time you're tempted to dress for Mardi Gras by dipping into Madonna's wardrobe, you've got to ask yourself: "Am I too old for this?" If you don't like that question, then ask yourself: "Is this too young for me? If I saw it on someone else in my age bracket, would I laugh?"

I have learned this truth in a painful way. More than once, I have bought a dress that I thought looked terrific on me, put it in my closet, and then my daughter Melissa would put it on and I'd say, "Oh, *that's* the look Lacroix (or Givenchy or Gaultier) was going for!"

Of course, I can still look pretty good; God knows, I try. But it is pretty good *for my age.* And I never try to fake it.

If you try to fake it, you'll fall on your unfashionable face. Nobody wants to see an older woman prancing around in badly cut peekaboo clothes. Remember the joke? I put on a peekaboo blouse. Well, a man peeked and then he booed.

Don't let this happen to you. Don't dress as if you're desperate for your youth. And, forgive me, but try not to look too trashy. True, men do like trashy, but remember, there's a line between a little trashy and TRASHY, and the woman over forty has to work hard to keep herself on the right side of that line—even if she has to put on her glasses to see it.

The essence of your wardrobe should be a simple black dress and two good suits. By "good" I don't mean that your clothes should come from only the most elegant shops; to dress well, you don't have to be rich. My own dresser and dear friend lives in a tiny Texas community. She buys half her clothes in Kmart—simple blazers, slacks, skirts, sweater sets—and she looks marvelous in them. Of course, she works hard to keep herself in shape. And you should too—or else you might have to get your outfits not at Kmart but at Home Depot.

"The best thing you can get," says Lauren Hutton, who has redefined a woman's fifties, "is a good blue blazer. It doesn't have to be Armani; J. Crew is fine. Also a simple white T-shirt will do wonders for you."

There are, of course, days when you feel you need not a fashion therapist but the whole Menninger Clinic. And certainly choosing what colors to wear can drive you in that direction. You want to wear a lot of black because it's chic and you feel that black will make it harder for people to locate your hips and your rear end. However, if black brings you down and makes you feel drab and you like the gaiety of color, you can also reap the benefits of color by wearing it as an accent, by accessorizing with it. A soft pink blouse under a black suit or a bright red hankie in the pocket of a navy blue blazer will add jolts of brightness.

And when it comes to accessorizing, don't forget jewelry. I have been in the jewelry business for nine years and I totally believe that wearing at least *one* piece of jewelry makes a woman look finished.

The important thing is to keep your jewelry

simple and appropriate. (If you're over thirty-five, a nose ring is not a good idea, unless you're planning to move to Borneo.) Just one pretty, artfully placed pin can pull a whole outfit together. It can, of course, be imitation, as long as *you're* real, as long as you know who you are and are happy with the identity.

Also think of your glasses as a necessary accessory. In fact, according to Lauren Hutton, they can actually be de-aging.

"Make them light, rimless if possible," she says, "and definitely small. Don't get glasses that cover your whole face."

There are mornings when I feel that those are precisely the kind of glasses I want, mornings when I think I should probably have some makeup help from Lon Chaney, so I choose sunglasses that are big and protective and definitely make the statement Greta Garbo made famous: "I vant to be alone."

Now let's get down to basics, those intimate little items in our arsenals that we can deploy to fight aging. Many models have told me that, after forty, you should start wearing control stockings as well as body shapers because at forty your body introduces itself to gravity and begins to head south.

Don't just watch it go. Put up stoplights. Call Control Central. Conjure up these tricks.

Introduce your torso to the Smoothie Diminish Minimizer Control. Don't laugh at the Smoothie, whose ads promise a "sleeker, slimmer, smoother you." In your battle against gravity, you will probably need not only the Smoothie, the Gripper, and the Huggie, but even lacy masking tape and maybe Ace bandages too, because parts of your body seem to be on ball bearings.

Gravity? Don't talk to me about gravity. When I get out of bed in the morning, I have to be careful not to step on my breasts.

However, until you need a full suit of armor to cover the fall of the body empire, I beg you to stock your lingerie drawer with silky, supple, sexy bras and panties and teddies. Don't just wear them on special occasions; make *every* day an occasion to don these undies, even if no one is likely to see them. Do it for yourself. It will make you feel good and make you feel sensuous; and if you feel sensuous, you'll act sensuously—and someone else *will* see those alluring undies after all.

On a less glamorous note, make sure they are also clean, for cleanliness can be a problem when people age. Because older people tend to be less careful about their grooming, you now have to be twice as fastidious at your toilette, just as you have to work twice as hard to stay your best in all other aspects of your life.

For example, no one should ever see hair growing out of a man's ears or nose or spot a mustache above a woman's upper lip or chin. And eyebrows! After a certain age, eyebrows tend to grow either up or down. You controlled your kids—well, some of the time. Do the same with your eyebrows!

And so, every morning take a good look at yourself in full daylight, if that's possible. Such a glimpse may be depressing, but people will be taking a good look at you for the rest of the day, and you want them to enjoy the view.

Yes, aging sucks, but the smart woman plucks.

Facial hair is something to be instantly eradicated any way you can, with tweezers, depilatory, electrolysis, laser, or waxing, but your crowning glory is another matter. Why is it that almost no one is happy with the head of hair nature has given her? If it's brunette, you want blond. Blond? You want auburn. Curly? You want straight. Straight? You want curls. Short? You're dying for long. Long? It's time to chop it off.

I look at my daughter, whose gorgeous silky hair cascades down to her shoulders. She wants it cut off!

"Melissa," I say, "you're crazy. Your hair looks great. Enjoy it while you can."

At my age, if I had long hair, I'd look like Miss Havisham from *Great Expectations*.

Yes, length of hair *is* key. Noted hairstylist Kenneth Battelle says that a woman's hair should be worn an inch shorter every few years. If this leaves you looking like a Marine when you're sixty-five, well, you'll be a stylish Marine.

You simply must accept the fact that long, long hair is now for your daughter, your son, or your dog. If you plan to always be walking away from people, then you can wear your hair down to your knees, but there is nothing more jarring than seeing a gorgeous head of hair from behind and then having it turn around to reveal a face that belongs on Mount Rushmore—if you *let* your face look like that.

While I know the value of short hair for my set (those who could use a little Three-in-One oil to get out of bed), I also know the dismay of another problem of age: thinning hair or balding. When this starts to happen, stop *teasing*. There is nothing worse than to be able to look through someone's hair—unless she's in front of you in a theater. I confess that I've had hair extensions from time to time and they're wonderful. Wigs too work miracles for the thinning-haired woman, as does that old television trick of subtly penciling in the scalp the same color as the hair that covers it. You'd be amazed how many TV beauties do this one! And don't forget Rogaine, transplants, and hair weaving—the same solutions available to balding men. And while we're on the subject, a balding man must never sweep hair from his temples across his shiny dome, unless he's in a Zero Mostel look-alike contest.

Moreover, when a man is over forty, his head should never be a retrospective. Every time I see a man of fifty with a ponytail, I realize that there are few things more depressing than an old hippie. Was there ever a bigger jerk than Timothy Leary at the end? By the time he was sixty, his trappings made us think that his message was out-of-date.

What about going gray? Gray or even white hair can be quite attractive, particularly if it isn't tinged with yellow. Just look at the chic editor of *Good Housekeeping*, Ellen Levine, who was gray before she turned forty and is now snow white.

However, if you don't like *your* gray, then go for a subtly soft warm color like butter-scotch or honey and not something gaudy like aquamarine. You don't want your head to look like the Caribbean. And never jet black either. Black from a bottle can be even more aging than gray.

Can you bear one more "never"? Never let

your hair be only one color. I'm a believer in highlights, though not the kind that pilots can see in the fog.

This wisdom applies not only to women but also to the weaker sex, for a man who takes a flier on the color wheel looks ludicrous too. From time to time, I see older men with orange hair, but there is something about orange hair that doesn't quite seem natural, unless the man happens to be an orangutan. No man should ever let himself go prematurely orange. Nothing dates him more.

With a woman, however, it's different. Kenneth Battelle says that it is usually a woman's makeup, not her hair, that dates her.

Many women a few decades shy of ninety continue to use makeup the way they did in their twenties: thin eyebrows or heavy eyeliner or thick mascara, or circles of rouge. They don't seem to know that there is an age when you have to stop wearing bright red lips or exaggerated lines under your eyes—and it makes no difference whether the lines have come from time or a tube.

There is nothing sadder than the sight of

the old Ziegfeld girls I occasionally see around New York: They are still wearing the thick stage makeup from a vanished yesterday. The clocks they carry in their heads have stopped in 1930, but *your* clock has to keep running on CST—Current Standard Time. You have to keep telling yourself: "I want to be part of the present world. I'm determined to live in the now."

In other words, wear makeup, but make sure it is today's makeup, not some stale remnant of an unchic yesteryear.

"But what about doe eyes?" you're saying.

"You mean the eyes you wore in the sixties?" I reply.

"Yes, but isn't there something timeless about them?"

"Absolutely. Timeless enough for the Smithsonian."

And even if doe eyes ever do come back, they would be trendy, and trendy is something you've got to keep a watchful (not doe) eye on, so swiftly do trends come and go. This warning comes not only from me, a cover girl for *Field and Stream,* but also from makeup expert Bobbi Brown of Bobbi Brown Essentials, whose other hip tips are worth writing on your bathroom mirror—but not with any lipstick color that's in the French flag. As the lady says:

"Your face loses some definition as it ages, so it's wrong for you to do nothing, but don't compensate with too *much* makeup. The older woman needs color, yes, but it must be soft. The only darkness should be your eyeliner and a bit of shadow on the lids. Definitely no *sparkles*."

In other words, save that Day-Glo mascara for your Barbie dolls.

Other beauty experts say that, as the shape around your eyes softens, more defining may be necessary, and so try keeping the intensity on your upper lash by using smudged shadows or lines while using a bit less on the under-eye area. There are mornings, of course, when what I need under my eyes (and over them too) is Wite-Out.

As for your lips, lining them not only will create a more defined shape but also will prevent bleeding of the color into those unsightly little cracks in your skin that stand like sentinels guarding your mouth. But relax: There are cosmetics that help stop the bleeding. Elizabeth Arden's Lip-Fix Cream applied over your lipline is a great one, as is Chanel's Levres color protector. As you know, lip color must be applied carefully and as indelibly as possible or you'll end up looking like my grandmother, who always seemed to have lipstick on at least one of her teeth.

In art, no principle is more fundamental than *less is more,* but this principle must be reversed when applied to the art of makeup. I am always amused when I hear a man say that a woman has a "natural" look. That means, of course, that she has applied her artifice well.

To help you out in this department, here are still more beauty tips for the mature woman (I guess that lets me out):

- Always use a lighted magnifying mirror when applying makeup.

- Pluck any stray hair that comes into your field of vision.

- Hit the bottle: Use plenty of moisturizer, even if your skin doesn't feel dry.

- Use concealer to camouflage any skin discoloration and shadows, especially under the eyes.

- Apply a yellow-toned foundation, not a heavy pink one that stops below the jawline. And blend in this foundation to "disappear" in your neck.

- Be sure to use blusher, not rouge, and smile while you apply it so it will be in the right places.

- Use a light touch. Caked-on makeup settles into fine lines and wrinkles. You don't want your face looking like a map of Pennsylvania.

- Give sparse eyebrows definition with a brow pencil, and if you're out of one, in a pinch use a regular pencil. Just avoid Magic Markers.

- Stay away from black mascara; it's very harsh. Instead try brown, which is also the best color for your eye shadow. Save the green, blue, and purple for a night at the circus.

- Use a soft, warm color on your lips, like apricot or rose or pink. Choose a deep purple or brown only if you want to look like a chic dead idiot.

- Have a manicure once a week and a pedicure at least monthly—even if you have to do it yourself. Grooming shouldn't stop at the neck.

- Wear any shade of nail enamel that strikes you as great, but black only if you're auditioning for the lead in *Irma Vep*.

- Become addicted to facials. Beauty schools give them free.

• Fall in love with the sensual pleasures of massage. Try them all: French full-body, Swedish, shiatsu—whatever turns you on.

• Get an herbal wrap, and a seaweed one too. It makes you feel totally detoxified.

• Treat yourself to the works at a day spa or a day-of-beauty salon.

If you still can't figure out what makeup will turn you into the best-looking woman of forty-eight in your house, go to the makeup counter of any department store and ask the experts there to make you over. Well, not *any* department store—Wal-Mart might not be able to do much for you, but free help *is* available at many places. Within a ten-block radius of where I'm now sitting in Manhattan, there are four: Bergdorf's, Bloomingdale's, Barney's, and Boyd's Pharmacy. And we're only up to the B's.

You can even go to a beauty school and volunteer to be a guinea pig, although guinea pig is a misnomer, for you almost certainly won't come out looking like the bride of Frankenstein. Some of my friends have had total makeovers at beauty schools—full makeup job and hair restyled, cut, body-waved, and colored—and they didn't have to enter the witness protection program. In fact, a couple of them never looked so gorgeous. And why not? Beauty schools are where all the biggies got their starts.

Now that I have filled you in on the essentials of wardrobe, hair, makeup, and style for a person your age, remember that there are no rules. It is all a matter of smart choices, of spending a hellishly long time facing yourself in the mirror and deciding how you look, how you *want* to look, and what you can do to look your best, and then making your picks from there—as an informed, aware, and vital mature woman.

Before we move on, however, let me lob you this zinger.

I have a friend, Elizabeth, who thought that she had wandered into a Salvador Dalí painting one day when she happened to meet a friend who was sixty. This woman was dressed not to the nines but the tens: a vinyl Chanel cap on her head of luxurious shoulder-length blond curls, a Gucci belt resting above slim hips at the point where her skimmy tank top from The Gap met her Escada short skirt. Then Elizabeth felt herself plunge even deeper into surrealism as she watched this woman sashay into Manolo Blahnik's and try on open-toed slingback heels.

However, Elizabeth confessed to me that the whole scene was surrealistic only because she *knew* the age of this woman, for actually the woman looked *nothing like a joke*. In fact, she looked terrific: not a line in her face, not a spider vein on a pair of legs that wouldn't quit, not a quiver of crepe dangling from the armhole of her top, and not an out-of-date piece of clothing on her thin, toned-up bod. This sixty-year-old broad was white hot and she looked it not only from the back but from the front too. She obviously had scrutinized herself, worked hard on herself, and fixed herself up in all the right places. And then she had sallied forth to make all the smart choices that keep her current.

Good for her! God knows what she'd gone through to look like that, but *it had worked*. An inspiration to us all: the saving of an endangered species. And the lesson is clear: Never give up.

How to Keep Current and Active

- Never stop for a rest between the bathroom and the bedroom.

- Chop down the tree where you and Abe Lincoln carved your initials.

- Run laps around someone even older than you.

- Have your dentist give you braces.

- Tell an old person, "Race you to the pharmacy!"

- Keep your body firm. Sleep in your freezer.

- Never admit that your back goes out more than you do.

FOUR

Early Plastic Isn't Chic

To be youthful after thirty-five, to be part of today's world and not Grover Cleveland's, it is not enough to have the right hairstyle, makeup, and dress: Your *home* must also be current and not a place that moves a guest to think, *Ah, a new wing of the American Museum of Natural History. I wonder what fossils are exhibited here. Oh, of course! Our hostess!*

Don't be the curator of a museum because you're too lazy or complacent to update your surroundings. Your house, as my mother used to say, is the frame for your picture. As you grow older, it's your duty to keep that picture current, bright, and cheerful, to make it reflect a place you're happy to come home to. Comfort is paramount, of course, but don't mistake comfort for dirty, shabby, tired, or worn—in other words, all the things that come to mind when you think of an old person's house, one that reeks of bygone good times, mothballs, or stale odors and musty smells.

Go instead for the sweet smell of today. Keep your place fresh. Air it out, let in the sunshine, let in the good aromas, burn scented candles, bake cookies, bake apples, and dab vanilla on the light bulbs. Fill your rooms with fragrant flowers and plants, and audaciously mix the fake with the real. It's a trick taught to me by my aunt, who mixed real flowers with fake greenery. The results were delightful.

I cannot tell you how important it is to keep your surroundings current. Yes, I can: It's very important. And one of the easiest ways to get your home to match the calendar is to constantly update your pictures. Display no photographs of Susan B. Anthony or Kaiser Wilhelm unless they're part of your family. And even if they *are* relatives, keep their faces in the background because no one wants to look only at a gallery of the dear departed. It is fine, of course, to have a nice shot of your grandfather smiling on the day of his arraignment, and it is fine to have a nice shot of your confirmation, when your most fervent prayer was to be rid of your baby fat, but you've also got to have some photos taken after Nixon's first term and some of new children too. Whenever there's a new baby in my family, even if I don't know who the father is, I display pictures of it.

But only one or two per child. No one wants to see thirty-seven pictures of your grandchild—which is also why you must never carry more than one picture of each grandchild in your wallet. All any self-respecting woman should have in her wallet are a few pictures and lots of credit cards. If someone really wants to see more grandchild photos, tell her to close her eyes and think of a very young Sharon Stone or Brad Pitt.

But let's get back to the photos that are on display. A friend of mine changes all the pictures in his house every four years so that everyone will look up-to-date. "I don't want to see me looking great nine years ago," he says.

Even with your beloved parents' photographs, you have to be careful that Mom isn't dressed like a flapper and Dad isn't waving goodbye from the deck of the *Titanic,* for nothing is a louder giveaway of *your* age than *their* pictures. How to avoid this problem? Always go for a close-up.

Whenever I've just come back from a trip, I put out the photos from that trip—unless, of course, it was to the Mayo Clinic. It's a way of updating your home to reflect your up-to-date life. Another of my tricks is to put current pictures on top of old ones, so that the past isn't really lost but neither is it hitting anyone in the face. Every time you glance at the frame, *you* know the history that's there behind the current snapshot.

It is pleasant, of course, to be reminded of the good things that have happened in our lives, but too strong a liking for nostalgia is often a sign that you are living in the past. And so, to confirm that you live in the present, show signs of it by keeping your home a reflection of today and not of the Civil War—in both photos and decor.

Before we even talk about decor, make sure that your house is sparkling clean because clean is young. Yes, your teenager's room looks like a toxic waste dump—well, perhaps it is not quite that neat. However, mess as a motif will not work for *you*. In fact, you should always try to keep your house freshly painted, for this is another way to keep it from looking like an old person's home. My grandmother's hallway had walls that looked like part of a Mayan temple.

Not only should you eliminate all the grimy and drab walls, but eliminate some of the furnishings too by periodically editing your home. As Thoreau used to say, "Simplify. Simplify." Of course, Thoreau didn't need an ornate place. Most of his guests were woodchucks.

At least once a year, go through all your possessions and try to eliminate some of the clutter that you have unknowingly built up. Then get your kids to come over and choose anything they love from that pile. What they don't want, give to Good Will, the Salvation Army, or your local thrift shop. Not only will this help keep you current, but you'll be able to take a tax deduction too. To make your home easier to edit, give it a slightly disposable tone. Don't furnish it with items so expensive that you'll have to go into therapy if a dog waters one of them.

Let me make one important thing clear: Keeping your home current is *not* a matter of calling for Martha Stewart or of tossing out all that old English furniture to make way for pared-down chrome or steel minimalism. Rather, it is having an awareness of where your life is *now* and doing something about it.

For example, if you happen to be an empty nester, if your kid has *really* left, then make his room into a nice guest room, study, library, den, office, or sewing room. Anything is better than keeping little Joey's room a shrine with his pennants on the wall and his Little League cup on the dresser, because little Joey is thirty-eight now, and when he comes home, he doesn't want to sleep in his little bunk bed.

Trust me, I know. At first my mother kept my room exactly as it was, and in the end, I wouldn't stay there. I would call and say, "I'm coming to Larchmont for the day, but after dinner, I'm going back to New York because I want to sleep in a grown-up bed in a grown-up's room." Although she said she understood, it still took her several years to turn my old bedroom into a real guest room, one that I happily stayed in, but in truth, she never truly could see how awful it can be to go through a house and find the kids' rooms still the way they were twenty years ago.

Another way to keep up-to-date is to sell the family manse that you've been rattling around in ever since little Joey and his siblings left and move to a smaller and totally different house or to an apartment. In fact, this may be the time to start all over again and to do it with a sense of adventure. Remember moving into your first apartment? Remember the thrill of it? The fun? Well, this could be just as exciting. As Yogi Berra would say, "Déjà vu all over again."

Wherever your house is located—city, country, or in between—consider it a work in progress, as opposed to your mother's or grandmother's home, where much of the furniture was done in Early Plastic Wrap.

When I was a girl, there were sofas and chairs in my home that my mother felt would have been damaged if people were thoughtless enough to sit on them. But when you consider your present age, this philosophy is idiotic. Sit on them, use them, enjoy them! Besides, you should never let yourself get so attached to a piece of furniture that you think you'll die if you have to replace it. Get attached to your husband if you want, but not to the chair in which he watches nine hours of Sunday football.

"Your home should age as gracefully as you," a top architect has told me. "Almost any period will do: Early American, Louis XV, Pre-Columbian, Danish Modern; they're all fine. But once you pick a period, stay with it."

In other words, if you want the Jurassic,

fine; but don't keep adding hip touches from the Cenozoic. (And don't do your house in any version of Japanese, or sometime soon after your sixtieth birthday, you'll find yourself needing a forklift to rise from those pillows.)

To mature with your home is one of the biggest challenges you face. If a friend says to you, "Your place hasn't changed in thirty years," you're not getting a compliment. Even a museum changes its exhibits.

Of course, just as you can age gracefully by not trying to look too cute in your clothes, you should also avoid an adorably dated design in your home. One friend of mine did her whole house in fifties kitsch, which would have been cute if her roommates had been Laverne and Shirley. You must realize that you simply cannot live in a time warp, no matter how appealing the rent may be.

For decorating tips, look at the decorating magazines the way you look at *Vogue* and *Harper's Bazaar* for your wardrobe, but don't be guided by elegant shelter magazines like *Architectural Digest* and *House and Garden*, which may lead you to buy a couch on which you will then have to lie down with a cold towel when you get the bill for it. Read the magazines that aren't furnishing East Hampton. And, just as with your wardrobe, be careful about being trendy. By the time a trend filters down to you, it may already be on its way out.

Having your home age gracefully is sometimes just a matter of rearranging the furniture, especially after a death in the family, and rehanging pictures works too. In fact, make a party of it: Ask some friends in to help, as in the painting parties of days gone by.

Of course, having your home age gracefully is *always* a matter of having it look fresh, with nothing worn out from a lifetime of use—especially *you*. It has to be a place where the residents look as though they're having fun. Again, especially you.

To keep your home up-to-date and fresh, remember that keeping current is in the details, the little touches. So:

- Keep one or two of the top ten best-sellers in your living room. You might even read them.

- Group six new photographs on one table.

- Treat your bed to designer coverlets and sheets.

- Buy new lampshades.

- Change to softer lighting, which is just a matter of changing bulbs.

- Always keep fresh towels in the bathroom.

- Buy three bright new tablecloths.

- Recover that stained and threadbare ottoman.

- Make sure that nothing is fake. Don't display a tennis racket if you don't play the game. Would you display a matador's cape?

- And always have fresh flowers somewhere and in *clean* water.

Best of all, get a pet, an animal you will love and one that will love you in return. In your home, there should be something besides the rugs to take care of. Get a pet that will stain those rugs and you'll have a happier home. Even if you're living with no one who happens to be a member of your species, your house has to contain *life*, for life in a house makes it happy and young. And mice don't count.

For the happiest of homes, you should fill it with people—young ones. And I don't mean just your children. They're a part of you, yes, but they have their own lives to live and you have yours, so don't make the mistake of living through them. Don't hound them daily to come and see you; don't give them the guilt your mother gave you. You know the routine:

"I'm lonely. I miss you. Nothing is happening."

I'm not suggesting that you shouldn't have your kids around from time to time, but also entertain other people's kids. Make friends with people who are younger than you, people in their twenties and thirties. It's great to have a mix of generations in your address book, and if you're a certain age, it's nice to look down a dinner table and see people who are out and functioning in the world. Moreover, younger friends will still be around to see you when members of your own generation have permanently departed.

"What," you might ask, "is in it for the younger people? Why would they want to gravitate to an old lady like me?"

Because, as Margaret Mead so well put it, "If you associate with older people who are enjoying their lives, you will gain a sense of continuity and the possibility for a full life."

From the days when he was a child star in Hollywood, Roddy McDowall always visited his older friends. I remember going to his house when there was a shaky but smiling Walter Pidgeon or Bette Davis at the table, who knew they were there because Roddy loved them. Roddy invited these oldies not out of charity but because they were his friends and because they contributed to the evening with wonderful stories, great wit, and wisdom.

I myself never give any kind of dinner party without mixing the age groups, and that's what keeps the conversation lively. I hope it is part of what makes my home a place to have fun in, and it can do the same for yours. Surrounding yourself with younger friends is the one surefire way to make your home a more interesting place.

Of course, you shouldn't want to hunker down there full time. I beseech you: Keep getting *out* of that home; go out every day. And I don't mean just to see your doctor. Don't make your hobby having medical checkups. Without realizing it, many women go from doctor to doctor just to be the center of attention, just to be listened to for a few minutes.

I'm not talking about therapists. If you feel you have to go to a therapist every day, by all means go. The talk—or cry, or sulk—will do you good, and so will the walk there and back.

No matter *what* you have to do to force yourself out of the house, do it! Get a job, if

you can, whether you need the money or not.
Make yourself have to show up at some bou-
tique three days a week. For the other days,
go to the Sisters of Charity and work in their
soup kitchen. And on rainy days, when you
say to yourself, "Oh nuts, why do I have to
go?" you'll know the answer: because going is
the price you have to pay to be involved in
the *now*. When you are in bed in your slinky
Natori, propped up against Porthault pillows
(okay, so they're knockoffs), atop your Beauty
Rest, I want you to write in a notebook three
good things that happened to you that day. I
want you to learn to appreciate your life and
be thankful for what God has given you. And
don't tell me that, even in the worst of times,
three good things haven't happened to you
today.

They can be as simple as, "I have a warm
winter coat" or "I have indoor plumbing" or
"My dog greeted me when I got home." Or "I
have a home." In even the worst of times, try
to see the good things that surround you.

This is just a nice way of counting your
blessings. And if you're whining about having

no blessings, then you'd better go out and find some. At this point in the book, you already *know* how to find them in your attitude, wardrobe, grooming, and home. Now it is time to let you be blessed in your fitness and health.

Good Things That Happened to You Today

- You woke up.

- You woke up without pain.

- You remembered you woke up without pain.

- You looked at the *New York Times* obituaries and you weren't there—again.

- You remembered at least half your children's names.

- You can still lift two ten-pound weights: your breasts.

- You covered every aisle in the twenty-nine-square-mile Wal-Mart without passing out.

- The drugstore just announced a 15 percent reduction on Ex-Lax.

- You have no real problems compared to your friends, especially the dead ones.

FIVE

Climb Every Staircase

Take HGH! Take DHEA! Take ZBT! Try shark liver oil! Try cod liver oil! Try Getty Oil!

There is now a feeding frenzy in America, and it isn't for food: It's for *supplements,* for vitamins, herbs, and hormones that will magically defeat aging and make us all healthy children again. Americans spend more than twenty billion dollars a year on unproven medical treatments. Just imagine what we would spend if we were sure that they worked. The claims, however, are irresistible.

For example, DHEA, as everyone knows,

stands for dehydroepiandrosterone, one of the steroid hormones, which is produced by the body until about the age of forty. The promoters of DHEA in pill form claim that artificial doses of it may do the following: restore youthful energy, sharpen your memory, build new muscle, insulate you against stress, combat cancer, burn body fat, hold off diabetes, improve your mood, increase your sex drive, ease menopause, erase wrinkles, moisten eyes, treat lupus, heal burns, stop bone loss, treat Alzheimer's disease, and increase longevity.

There is, however, no claim that it also does windows.

The promoters of HGH (human growth hormone) have a similar list: It will do everything but put you in the NBA.

Well, here's the catch: As yet, there has been no valid, long-term testing of the effects of these hormones and herbs on people. They may put mice in wonderful shape, but we don't know what high doses of them for long periods do to the human body. DHEA, for example, increases the body's production of estrogen and testosterone, hormones that, when taken in excess, can increase your chance of developing certain cancers, and HGH can lead not only to diabetes and high blood pressure but also to breast, colon, and prostate cancer.

Your road to good health shouldn't be leading you off a cliff.

Late last year on the *CBS Evening News,* Dan Rather reminded Americans that all of the most popular hormone replacement regimens—DHEA, HGH, testosterone, estrogen, and progesterone—still have not been fully tested in human beings.

However, women have reason to be optimistic in considering estrogen, for medical researchers are now hard at work developing a so-called designer estrogen that will be good for bones and also prevent coronaries and breast cancer while not increasing the risk of uterine cancer. The two drugs being studied are tamoxifen and raloxifene. Conclusive results are only a year or two away.

But what should you do if you happen to be postmenopausal right now?

(Of course, you feel grateful that you have finally survived the ordeal, even if you do keep complaining about hot flashes so that people will think you're as young as you've made yourself feel.) Well, you must make a choice, and it should be an informed one: You've got to weigh the risks of the currently available hormone replacement therapy (the estrogen-progesterone combination) against its benefits. Do you want an increased risk of getting uterine cancer and possible cancer of the breast in exchange for lowering your risk of coronary disease and osteoporosis, while also remaining more youthful and well lubricated and possibly still getting your period as proof of your youth?

I have a friend who is seventy and I hear her say to her younger husband, "It's time for me to take my birth control pill." And, smiling proudly, he says to me, "Isn't it wonderful? She still gets her period!" Of course, the pills that she's taking have nothing to do with birth control: They're the hormone replacements Premarin and Provera, which do indeed cause bleeding every month. But why enlighten him? The two of them are happy in their ovarian fantasy.

Another friend of mine, a dancer, was headed for a really big breakdown at menopause.

"I'm over the hill," she sobbed. "It's over for me."

But then her doctor said that he could extend her period forever so she wouldn't feel old, and she said, "Great." Like millions of other women, she went on hormone replacement therapy. Nine years later, she's still dancing, even, as she proudly puts it, "on days when I have my visitor."

If that's what will make you happy, don't let anyone dissuade you—not your doctor, your mother, your friends, or *New York Times* health columnist Jane Brody, but do be aware of Brody's words:

"Because none of the new anti-aging hormones has been properly tested, the eventual side effects could be damaging and even deadly. There are no long term studies of either the benefits or risks of these hormones. Most of the claims for them are based on studies in mice and rats."

In other words, if you take too much of one of these hormones, your aging might be stopped prematurely. But at your wake, you'll have a youthful glow.

There is even a new antiwrinkle treatment called Botox that injects weakened botulism (at full strength, one of the deadliest poisons) into facial muscles to paralyze them and thus smooth out the skin. I've had Botox done and it's great: no more full face wrinkles when I smile. True, it is voluntary muscular paralysis from a poisoned Fountain of Youth, and if the needle hits the wrong muscle, I can't close my eyes. Oh, well, I'll be awake for only six months because then the treatment wears off and beauty demands fresh paralysis.

There is also the potentially lethal fen-phen, the supposedly miraculous diet pill that was pulled off the market last year because it was suspected of causing fatal heart defects. But don't let that particular recall lull you into a false sense of security. According to Dr. Louis Aronne, director of the Comprehensive Weight Control Program at New York Hospital–Cornell Medical Center, "Some of the other herbal products [that are available at so-called health emporiums] contain ingredients that are more likely to kill you than fen-phen."

A few years ago, the House of Representatives Subcommittee on Health and Long-Term Care issued a report called *Quackery: A Twenty Billion Dollar Business,* which spelled out all the ways that Americans spend money on medical treatments that belong on a boardwalk. When P. T. Barnum said, "There's a sucker born every minute," he was talking about the U.S. of A.—the Unlimited Suckers of America. Want to sell the eye of a newt as a cure for gout? Sell it to an American. Want to sell peat moss to grow hair? Your market is Yankee Doodle dopes.

Bernadette Marriott of the National Institutes of Health says, "Many herbs have traditionally been used for a short period of time, but now people are taking them for a longer duration and we really don't know the impact."

I can tell you the impact: Herb profits go up.

As of 1998, the only *certain* paths to health and longevity are *regular exercise* and a *balanced diet*. Boring but true.

The proof of this truth is overwhelming. For example, in 1982 a man of seventy-five named Sam Gadless was suffering from arthritis, high cholesterol, high blood pressure, and diabetes.

"Then I changed my diet and started to walk," Sam says. "Now I'm always walking."

Except when he's running: Sam has competed in eleven marathons (you channel surfers may not know that a marathon is twenty-six miles, 385 yards), and he has broken the world record for the five-kilometer race walk for age eighty and over.

Sam Gadless ran the 1998 New York Marathon at the age of ninety-one, and you're complaining that the cab couldn't drop you in the middle of the block.

In one town in South Carolina, a group of men play softball every Tuesday afternoon. Their average age is approximately the average temperature: seventy-six. A couple of them have pacemakers, but what's saving their lives is the pace of the Tuesday afternoon game.

"It only hurts when I don't play," said one of these boys of winter a few days after he had turned eighty.

"At the age of one hundred," says Jack LaLanne, "day laborers in China are *still* doing what they did all their lives because they never stopped."

They have a lousy union, but they are certainly in shape!

Use it or lose it.

Those may be the five most important words you'll ever hear, even more important than "You're not in the will." Paste them to the door of your shower, where every day you see the body you would like to recycle, and paste them to the door of your refrigerator, where you keep your hip enhancers.

Aware that *use it or lose it* is the best single guide to a long, healthy life, I try to exercise one hour every day and I do it at home, where only my dogs can laugh at me.

First, I walk two miles on a treadmill, and then I do vigorous exercises for my upper body (whatever is still left up there) and my upper arms—and still they look like something flapping on a clothesline. A woman my age—I forget what age that is—has to fight every day to keep her arms from looking like wrinkled laundry, and she also has to fight every day to keep her thighs from looking like something half blown up in the Macy parade.

"Has a soft and wavy frame like the silhouette of a dame," the sailors sing in *South Pacific,* but nearly everyone has to work to avoid a full-of-gravy frame, and the best way to do it is with exercise. So get yourself off to Pilates at once. Or if, like me, you're timid about working out in a gym, know that you can still exercise nicely by yourself at home with just the equipment you had as a child. An average person of about 150 pounds uses up about 350 calories in a half-hour of jumping rope. You feel a half-hour of jumping rope is *hard*? You're right. It's a lot easier to relax and have a stroke.

Many other objects found in any household can do wonders to keep you in shape without your leaving the comfort of home. Water bottles, for example, can double as weights; thick rubber bands work well for resistance; and for push-ups, sit-ups, and stretching, all you need is the floor. Yes, so many exercises need no equipment at all, like isometrics and the Royal Canadian Air Force workout, which is right for men and women of all ages.

Any exercise at any time is a plus—and for most of us, it should be a must. Do I sound like Richard Simmons? Well, I have better legs, and at least they've maintained their altitude, unlike certain other parts of me. I feel the way Gypsy Rose Lee did when she said, "I have everything I had twenty years ago, only it's a little lower."

In an effort to keep up what's still up, whenever there are stairs in a building, I try to climb them instead of taking an escalator or elevator. Kenneth, my hairdresser, is three flights up, and I always walk those flights. It's hardly a trek up Everest, but it does give me a kind of low high.

As for elevators, whenever you can, avoid them. I'm not talking about a trip to the top of the World Trade Center, of course, or even to the tenth floor. However, for lower floors, try to walk as many stairs as you can. Push yourself to the point where you are slightly out of breath but can still carry on a conversation. Think of yourself as sounding a little like Marilyn Monroe.

In your fight to stay fit, think of stairs—both up and down—as your staunchest ally: Up builds muscle, down builds bone. And you gain a defense against obesity, which seems to be the single most popular look in America. The latest figures on American obesity are appalling: *Fifty-five percent of adult Americans are overweight!* We are a land of plenty, and you can see this plenty on our stomachs, hips, and behinds. We sit in front of the computer, in front of the TV, in front of the fridge—when we should be walking, walking, walking.

I was particularly aware of American sedentary flab last year when I took a trip to Kenya, where exercise gurus would be talking to themselves because nobody there needs their message. In fact, incredibly, I didn't see one fat person in Kenya. I traveled among the

Masai, all of whom are thin, and not because they're bulimic. They simply walk everywhere. As we fat Americans drove past them, they struck me as so lean and beautiful.

If you're creative, you can find many chances to walk in your daily routine. For example, if you do have to take a taxi for an appointment, tell the driver to drop you off a block or two from your destination. In New York City these days, many drivers will cooperate with your exercise program by dropping you even more than a block or two away because they are best at finding addresses in downtown Baghdad.

And no matter where a taxi leaves me, I always carry my own luggage to build up my back and upper body. These days, when men behold me, they say, "Lovely. She looks like a woman who carries her own luggage."

If you're taking a bus, put yourself in situations where you have to run to catch it. And then, when you get on, maybe some convalescent won't be offering you her seat. You burn more calories standing than sitting.

Always look for ways to keep your body

moving—and not just during sex. (*That*, in fact, is when I sometimes doze off.) Park your car at the farthest spot in the lot and walk briskly to the store. *Walk* to the hairdresser, to the market, and to the movies; walk even when you're on the phone; and *walk* on the golf course: Don't commute to the holes. If you do play golf, a game that barely qualifies as exercise, stay off the carts, unless you're going for pizza. And here's a way to really intensify things: Carry your own clubs or at least wheel them.

In walking for your health, move as quickly as you can and keep your head up and pump your arms. Cardiovascular exercise counts as exercise *only* if it raises the pulse; so, if the exercise you choose is walking, try for a pace of at least three miles an hour, roughly the speed of a car in New York rush hour traffic. Want to be healthy for a long time? Then be a street walker, not a channel surfer.

The ideal exercise for people over forty is twenty to thirty minutes of brisk walking three or four times a week. Remember: Walking raises your heart rate but doesn't lower your bank account because no expensive equipment is needed—just two legs and one strong will, and the sense not to do it on Rodeo Drive.

A twelve-year study of 707 men at the University of Virginia School of Medicine revealed that 13.3 percent of those who had walked less than a mile a day had died of cancer versus 5.3 percent of those who had walked at least two miles a day, and the rate of death from heart disease was 6.6 percent for those who had walked the least and 2.1 percent for those who had walked the most.

And a study at the University of Helsinki of sixteen thousand men and women, all identical or fraternal twins, revealed that a brisk half-hour walk just six times a month can cut your risk of death almost in half. Twins who exercised the equivalent of a vigorous thirty-six-minute walk six times a month had a 44 percent lower risk of death than a sedentary brother or sister. Nature *meant* for us to walk. It's the Ford Motor Company that meant for us to ride.

I think I'm going to change my favorite question to "Can we *walk*?"

Yes, every bit of research reveals the same thing: Even if you have bad genes, increasing your physical activity can help you live longer. Most members of the medical profession now say that your genes are responsible for no more than 30 percent of your health. The other 70 percent is up to *you* and cannot be blamed on your mother and father. You can blame them for throwing away the comic books that sell for thousands today, but not for your physical condition.

Are you *really* aware of what exercise can do for you at *any* age? Are you aware of what it can do for your *brain*? After testing thousands of older people for twenty years, researchers at Harvard have discovered that vigorous exercise enhances mental function by keeping the lungs and blood vessels healthy, thus increasing the flow of oxygen-rich blood to the brain. And, as we all know from Biology 101, oxygen-rich blood is the single most important nutrient to feed the brain and stimulate it to work at peak performance. And you always thought the best brain food was fish!

In another study in 1994, at a nursing home

near Boston, one hundred frail residents, some as old as ninety-eight, were given high-resistance strength training by researchers from Tufts University.

"How many did it kill?" you're asking.

What it killed was senility. The residents were put through a series of strengthening exercises on machines three times a week for eight weeks. The results were marvelous and hard to believe.

The residents increased their strength, their balance, and their walking speed; in fact, they *doubled* the strength of their quadriceps, the major thigh muscle. Many of them began to walk at *three times* their previous speed, all shuffling was ended (except for shuffleboard), and everyone managed to remain vertical. Life can be quite pleasant when you're not periodically falling down.

Moreover, the Tufts researchers say that such exercise can increase the bone density of postmenopausal women, even if they are not taking estrogen. And for both sexes, exercise increases muscle tone and stamina, lowers cholesterol, and provides innumerable other benefits that slow down aging and also help you look and feel younger. In fact, exercise not only strengthens the muscles you have but also causes new ones to be formed—which is why I am writing this on a treadmill.

If Ponce de León had only known that the Fountain of Youth was not a Florida geyser but a Florida gym.

If you don't have the time or inclination to do structured exercising at a gym, at a health club, or in your bedroom, you can turn cleaning your house into an aerobics workout by vacuuming strenuously for thirty minutes or by walking briskly around the house for thirty minutes, perhaps dusting as you go. How do you think Mary Poppins avoided cellulite?

No matter how much fun thirty minutes of vacuuming might be, I much prefer to walk. And because I walk a lot and seek out stairs and take half-rides in cabs, I passed a recent stress test magna cum laude: I did more than ten minutes at phase four, leaving my trainer incredulous and leaving me feeling as though I had just climbed a mountain. I have never taken drugs— an Excedrin high is the best I can do—but I cannot imagine a chemical high to equal the intoxication of an hour of vigorous exercise, and I feel, as you should, that I always can do even *more*.

For years, doctors have been saying that the average human being uses only 10 or 20 percent of his total physical and mental capacity. Some of the people I've known in show business were mentally at 10 percent, and that probably was their limit, but most of us can go higher with both our bodies and our minds. Robert Browning may have gone blank when he said the best is yet to come, but he did get it right when he said:

A man's reach should exceed his grasp
Or what's a heaven for?

Of course, his wife, Elizabeth, should have made him add:

A woman needs no heavenly plan
To reach as far as any man.

People are forever being told to "act their age," but the role no longer comes with stage directions. When John Glenn went back into orbit last fall at the age of seventy-seven, what role was *he* acting? And was legendary Broadway director George Abbott acting 105 when, at that age, he was still telling performers how to act their parts?

The Bible is a magnificently timeless book, but one of its lines needs updating: *The age of man is threescore years and ten*. Well, seventy may have been a senior citizen when Moses was founding the AARP (the August Association of Retired Prophets), but to Dr. Kenneth Cooper, founder of the Cooper Aerobics Center in Dallas, seventy is just his pulse one minute after a workout.

Dr. Cooper remembers being taught in medical school that vigorous exercise after forty increased the risk of a heart attack. His teacher must have been the same mother who told children not to swim right after a meal, a tip that makes sense only if they're swimming with sharks, for food followed by swimming does not cause cramps. Now, at sixty-seven, Dr. Cooper runs or race-walks several times a week, lifts weights, skis at least two weeks a year, and climbs a thirteen-thousand-foot peak in the Rockies every summer.

"The effects of aging can not only be slowed but actually reversed," he says, "through a diet-and-fitness regimen that strengthens bones and builds muscle mass. We are eventually going to rewrite the textbook on aging."

Eventually may be coming soon, for there are now fifty thousand people over one hundred in America, and in the next twenty-five to fifty years, American life expectancy will increase by ten to fifteen years.

Elizabeth Arden of Red Door fame always claimed never to be interested in age.

"People who tell me their age are silly," she used to say. "You're as old as you feel."

Did George Bush feel his age when he redefined seventy-two with a *parachute jump*? About the same time Bush was dropping from that plane, a retailing executive named Al Dietzel made a jump on his sixty-fifth birthday, right after eighteen holes of golf (no cart, of course), two sets of singles tennis, a 180-pound bench press, and a two-mile run at a nine-mile-a-minute pace. What particular age was he acting?

Was Al Dietzel born on Krypton? Has he been pouring steroids on his cornflakes? No, he is just a man who knows that the great rejuvenator is vigorous exercise and not chewing your way through a health food store.

"I'm stronger at sixty-six," he says today, "than I ever was in my life."

In a book called *Fitness Is Religion*, Madonna's personal trainer, Ray Kybartas, tells us that exercise has seven different benefits: an improved quality of life, a slowing down of the aging process, improved psychological health, consistent weight control, improved cardiovascular health, increased strength and muscle mass, and improved body chemistry.

Leave it to the Beaver, Jerry Mathers, to sum up this wisdom after saving his own life by dramatically losing fifty pounds, for he also had diabetes and high blood pressure.

"Exercise and portion control," he says, now limiting his meals after becoming a happy portion of his former self.

Yes, exercise is half the formula for the Fountain of Youth. Now let's take a hard look at the *other* half.

The Good Things About Menopause

- You don't have to worry about getting your period in the middle of hockey practice.

- You never have to shave your legs. The heat will melt your hair off.

- You can roast a chicken by setting it in your lap.

- When you get night sweats, bring shampoo to bed and wash your hair.

- At last, you have a legitimate reason to complain.

SIX

Some People Will Swallow Anything

The other half, as the Beaver said, is a sensible diet. However, following a diet in America can be as hard as scaling Dr. Cooper's peak, for all of us know that everything delicious is fattening. In fact, it was Socrates who said, "Hemlock isn't so bad. It could have been diet cola."

When it is cold and fresh, diet cola still tastes like liquid rust. And have you ever tried low-fat cream cheese? Almost as tasty as library paste. Fat in food was clearly invented by Satan, for the awful truth is that there isn't one dish known to man that doesn't taste worse when the fat is left out.

And so, healthful eating demands the discipline of Al Dietzel's private Olympics. Some people say that you've got to weigh yourself *every day* and not wait until you have gained ten or fifteen pounds. The Duchess of Windsor weighed herself every morning (she didn't have much else to do), and if she saw that she had gained even one pound, she didn't eat that day.

Well, that strategy is fine if you want to look like a frail waif at ninety, but I have a better trick: Hide the scale and do once-a-week weigh-ins. The reason? A scale that hasn't gone up gives you permission to eat.

My own diet involves the constant removal of temptation. For example, whenever I eat in a restaurant, I never let the waiter leave bread on the table. If it sits on the table, I'm going to eat it because, like Oscar Wilde, I can resist everything but temptation. And so I am responsible for the only waiters who have ever returned an entire basket of bread to the kitchen.

"Doesn't that bitch like the way we sliced it?" one of the chefs once said.

I do let the waiter give me water because I try to drink more than a gallon of water every day. Going soggy is good for the body and good for the skin. Gloria Vanderbilt also drinks water all day, but hers is Evian and mine is often essence of Hudson.

At breakfast, my biggest meal, I play a different game with myself: I start off with fruit, which fills me enough not to be starving when I start on the bacon, eggs, toast, jam, Danish—anything I want, and I stop when I'm full. For the rest of the day and night, I ration my food. However, once in a while, I do let myself indulge, and my indulgence is never broccoli: It is fruitcake or carrot cake or brownies or anything that has an icing. If shoes came with icing, I'd be barefoot.

Dieting isn't pleasant or easy, but nothing worthwhile is, and the results of sensible eating—slimness, health, and longevity—are at the top of life's worthwhile list, even above repositioning your breasts so they point to the horizon again. I have even gone so far as to flush down the toilet fattening food that slipped into my house by mistake. Yes, I am the woman responsible for sweetening the sewers of New York.

I have always been amused by the publication of a new diet book every ninety minutes in America. Dr. Atkins's Diet, Dr. Tarnower's Diet, Dr. Ulene's Diet, Dr. Brady's Diet, Dr. Arnot's Diet, Dr. Conner's Diet, Dr. Seuss's Diet—I think only my podiatrist has missed this bandwagon. And yet, in spite of all this authoritative gab about flab, one-third of all Americans continue to live in Fat City. Well, my only degree is a B.A. from Barnard College, but I do happen to know a diet that is more effective than any of these, although it might not make a book because it doesn't make a paragraph:

Stop eating so damn much.

We love to say that the most American things are Mom, baseball, and apple pie. We do not say, however, that every third Mom looks like a beach ball because she always has two pieces of apple pie á la mode, after which she moves like the *Hindenburg* to the living room. According to the National Center for Health Statistics, the average American woman is now five feet, four inches tall and weighs 144 pounds—twenty pounds more than the average American woman did a decade ago. This, not the economic index, is America's most alarming rate of inflation.

Take a good look at typical aging Americans, and what do you see? Many people are sloppily fat because of a total lack of discipline, because they've given up, because they feel they're old and think, *Why bother? I've had my kids and no one's going to look at me anyhow, so I might as well enjoy myself with food.*

Well, they're wrong. No matter what your age may be, no matter how old you feel you are, you should want to look the best you can for that moment. So make the moments count: Be proud of yourself and be aware that part of that pride is keeping fit and looking great—and that a big part of looking great is *not* being fat.

Except for playing with asbestos, no health hazard is greater than obesity. Doctors used to say that obesity was one contributing factor in premature death. Last June, however, this view was revised: Doctors now say that obesity is the *major factor* in premature death because it can lead to so many different causes of death: heart attack, diabetes, cancer, and stroke, to say nothing of your being laughed to death in Bermuda shorts.

Yes, buried in those causes, you saw the word "cancer." A 1997 Harvard study revealed that if a woman is more than twenty pounds overweight, her risk of breast cancer is doubled because the extra weight produces too much estrogen. Estrogen makes us feminine, but too much can make us disappear.

Another study last year, of twenty-eight thousand women, found that those who lost twenty pounds were 20 percent more likely to stay alive in the next twelve years than those who had lost no weight.

"Until this study, there was no direct evidence that losing weight would improve your longevity," says the study's head, Dr. David F. Williamson of the Centers for Disease Control and Prevention in Atlanta. One of the things I like about Dr. Williamson is that he hasn't written a diet book.

I can't resist telling you about the only diet I've ever known that will always work for everyone. It was used about forty years ago by the great light-heavyweight boxer Archie Moore, who often had to lose twenty or thirty pounds in just a few weeks before a fight. To drop this weight so quickly, Archie continued putting lots of food in his mouth; however, he wisely knew that what gets an eater in trouble is the *swallowing*. And so he swallowed all the juices for their nutritional value, but he spat out all their solid sources.

Needless to say, Archie was never the hit of dinner parties—hostesses wanted less of Moore—but he did know the only infallible diet: *Eat all you want. Just don't swallow.*

The important thing to remember is that you control your food portions, whether or not you eat regularly throughout the day or wolf down one huge meal each evening. Many of us don't realize that we are in charge of our feeding; it is nonsense to blame our genes and say, "I was born to be fat." That line makes sense when spoken by a hippo, but when *people* eat less, there is less of them. There is no Weight Watchers in Calcutta. Sorry to strike that grim note, but too many of us are committing leisurely suicide with knives and forks.

Another doctor who didn't write a book, Dr. Samuel Johnson, said that an eater should always leave the table before he is full. He may have been misquoted, of course, because Johnson himself looked as though he might have needed a tugboat to leave the table, but the point is still sound. Four small meals a day are more healthful than two huge ones; and two small meals would be even better, for experiments with monkeys have revealed that reduced eating decreases the rate of aging from 25 to 50 percent. Give an ape a salad for lunch instead of fifty bananas and he'll be swinging around for a long time. Other experiments have shown that underfed rats live 50 percent longer than rats that eat more, and the basic aging processes of all mammals are similar.

"But are those rats happy?" you're asking

me. "They may be missing a certain quality of life."

Maybe you're also thinking that *you'd* rather not be hungry for ninety-five years. And maybe you're thinking that there is just too much conflicting and uncertain information about diet. Well, except for the indisputable truth about the value of eating less, you're right.

Sometimes it seems that dining intravenously is the only safe way to eat in a nation whose doctors keep changing their minds about which foods are poison and which poisons are food. For example, about fifteen years ago, I switched from butter to margarine when doctors said that if I kept on eating butter, I would soon need Drāno for my arteries. About 1990, however, the doctors announced that the total fat content of margarine was roughly the same as butter. *Possibly* the same. Or maybe *not*.

"Just one serving of fish a week seems to cut in half the risk of sudden cardiac death," says the *Journal of the American Medical Association*. However, the *JAMA* goes on to say that other studies have shown that fat from fish may increase the risk of breast cancer 69 percent.

The confusion extends in all directions and to the foods we love most. For many years, science believed that chocolate caused headaches. Last year, however, medical researchers finally decided it doesn't. In fact, not only is chocolate not harmful, but last year *USA Weekend* reported that researchers at the University of California at San Diego found that chocolate has benefits never dreamed of: It boosts the "feel good" chemicals in the brain (endorphins and serotonin), thus promoting euphoria and calm, as some women have found when using chocolate to fight PMS; it helps to control blood sugar. Moreover, tests have shown that chocolate may *discourage,* not promote, tooth decay! It contains the same disease-fighting "phenolic" chemicals as fruits, vegetables, and red wine.

Can you take two more sweet stunners? Chocolate does *not* cause acne and it does *not* cause hyperactivity! And, unlike penicillin, you need no prescription for M&Ms.

Although there is no longer any doubt about the benefits of chocolate, other goodies keep moving in and out of the sun. In 1997, it was revealed that alcohol is good for your heart. In 1998, however, it was revealed that alcohol might cause breast cancer, and also cancer of the colon, tongue, throat, and esophagus. In 1999, it may be revealed that alcohol is the best thing to relieve the symptoms caused by reading the medical news.

It's all so bewildering.

As another example, last year, in a bulletin that could have come from the medical wing of the rabbit hole, it was revealed that low cholesterol might actually be *bad* for you. A new study, undoubtedly conducted by the Mock Turtle, found that men with low cholesterol were more likely to die violently—by suicide, accident, and murder—than were men with high cholesterol. However, since *high* cholesterol can kill you too, I figure the only answer is to have *no* cholesterol.

To be serious about it, as your doctor can explain, there are two kinds of cholesterol: the good cholesterol, called HDL for high-density lipoprotein, which helps cleanse the arteries; and the bad cholesterol, called LDL, for low-density lipoprotein, which clogs them. Good luck in keeping track of the two.

And there is still more to dismay the seeker of good health. In March 1998, it was revealed that olestra, the highly touted fat substitute, drains important nutrients from the body, may block natural digestion, and may cause diarrhea and frequent urination.

That same month, another study showed that low-salt diets might be dangerous.

"For those on a low sodium diet," said Dr. Michael Alderman in *The Lancet,* a British medical journal, "harm may outweigh benefit."

However, just *five days* after the publication of this story, another study said that low-salt diets are wonderful, lowering high blood pressure enough to help some people get off medication—the medication they might have started to protect themselves against both salt and medical studies.

"Why can't the researchers ever get it right the first time?" I am sometimes asked at my lectures. "What are we supposed to *do*?"

Yes, what was *I* supposed to do ten years ago when the bad news came out about margarine? Go back to butter or switch to axle grease? I had been playing kitchen roulette, nervously looking for a spread that didn't require an antidote.

Meanwhile, my husband, Edgar, was brooding about a new report on spinach. He and I had grown up thinking that spinach was the road to eternal life—we had heard this great truth from the same mothers who had told us not to go swimming right after a meal—but then a doctor had told Edgar, "You know, too much spinach can give you an excess of oxalic acid and cause kidney stones. Popeye was asking for a big urology bill."

About a year ago, in a healthier-than-thou tone, I happened to see this same doctor and I said to him, "You'll be happy to know that I'm eating a lot of yolkless fried egg sandwiches and low-fat milk with chocolate syrup."

"Well, chocolate does have caffeine," he said, "and caffeine has affected the behavior of mice. And I remember Edgar telling me that you put a lot of *salt* on your eggs. That can raise your blood pressure, you know."

"I just read a story that says that chocolate is better than antibiotics," I said, "and another story that said salt is *okay*. This week, I mean."

"Not for people sensitive to it," the doctor replied. "In northern Japan, they eat four times the salt that we do and have the world's highest rate of hypertension. But in America, where we consume less, it still isn't clear if we should watch our intake."

"So salt isn't as clear-cut a danger as cholesterol?"

"Who says cholesterol's a clear-cut danger?"

"Everyone over the age of *six*," I said.

"But most of the research has been done on middle-aged men," he told me. "To women, cholesterol may be mother's milk."

"Well, there's *one* thing that's certainly good: At least I never eat *bacon fat*. I don't want my circulatory system turned into an obstacle course."

"Oh, it's less the fat in bacon than the sodium nitrite. No one really knows what sodium nitrite can do."

"Would you be happier if I told you that I'm heavily insured?"

In the following days, I desperately sought validation for my diet. In one cookbook, I happily confirmed the *USA Weekend* story by discovering that the Aztecs had loved chocolate, and they had flourished for hundreds of years. I did wonder, however, if all that chocolate had left them mellow even when they were tossing virgins into volcanoes.

A few weeks later at breakfast, a friend said, "I have to change my coffee and go back to caffeine. A new study says that decaffeinated coffee drinkers have higher levels of cholesterol than regular coffee drinkers."

"Were they northern Japanese or suburban Aztecs?" I said.

How much longer could my tiny layman's brain keep trying to make sense of constantly changing reports from the world of medicine? Were there *no* absolutes left? Was I about to learn that the human body required a minimum daily dose of carbon monoxide?

In dismay, I stopped eating margarine as well as butter and red meat and I began eating oat bran muffins, pretending they didn't taste like Styrofoam. I also switched to no-nitrite bacon, thus lowering my cholesterol and possibly my IQ too. For the next few weeks, I felt like a winner at kitchen roulette. And then I made the mistake of opening a newspaper and reading the conclusion of a new report: There was no conclusive proof that eating oat bran lowered cholesterol.

And so I've dispelled my culinary confusion by playing it safe across the board and trying to eat just the minimum at meals, a diet that I deeply believe will keep me both healthy and thin—until, of course, someday some doctor will discover that *overeating* increases longevity in chimpanzees.

Not only do I eat the smallest possible portions, but I enforce my dieting with a fashion trick: Whenever I lose a couple of pounds, I take in all my clothes at once so I will have no wardrobe if I gain the weight back. I urge you to do the same thing: Leave yourself with only a towel to wear if you gain the weight back. And if you absolutely cannot keep from gaining weight, then join Overeaters Anonymous, an organization as good as AA, and draw strength from fellow stuffers.

"Hi, I'm Allison and I eat anything that isn't moving."

"*Hi,* Allison! Have a radish."

A friend once told me what a lift she got from hearing a woman at Overeaters Anonymous confess that she *also* retrieved food from her garbage can and ate it after having thrown it away.

But that thought gives me no lift, for it underscores what a nation of scary overeaters we are. All over the world, people are taking food from garbage cans, but only in America are they taking back their own.

"Suppose I replace food with vitamins?" you may be wondering. "That would keep me thin and fight aging too."

The answer is that a balanced diet usually gives you all the vitamins you need, although certain vitamins in pill form are helpful for certain conditions, like vitamin C for weak gums. And a few months ago, it was revealed that folic acid and vitamin B$_6$ can cut a woman's risk of a heart attack by 50 percent. But must you get these elements in *pills*? No: Both exist naturally in foods.

Americans, to whom "moderation" is a foreign word, are swallowing vitamins as if they were peanuts, unaware that massive doses can activate your eulogy. Too much vitamin A, for example, can put you in line for a liver transplant.

"I took too much niacin," a woman recently said on TV, "and I thought my skin was on fire."

Like the ancient Persians, too many of us today are seeking immortality in a bottle, but the genie now comes from Squibb.

Some of these bottles contain antioxidants to fight what are called free radicals. The current theory of why we age is that the cells of our bodies are attacked by free radicals. I had always thought a free radical was a Communist on parole, but I have learned that it's a loose cannon of a molecule that damages us after forty and promotes aging and disease.

Incredibly, last April, British researchers at the University of Leicester found that a five-hundred-milligram supplement of vitamin C had pro-oxidant as well as anti-oxidant effects, promoting genetic damage by free radicals as well as protection from them.

"It's an antioxidant in some circumstances and a pro-oxidant in others," said Dr. Victor Herbert of New York's Mount Sinai Medical School.

In other words, if you are lucky, your recommended daily dosage of vitamin C will be happily self-canceling and give you all the protection of a Tic-Tac. A remarkable pill: the poison and the antidote all in one. The C clearly stands for cockamamy.

Of course, following a good diet may be all you need to combat free radicals and stall aging and disease. I wish I could tell you that the best free radical fighters were caramel custard and key lime pie, but fruits and vegetables have the most antioxidants, especially avocados, berries, carrots, citrus fruits, grapes, onions, spinach, tomatoes, broccoli, and cabbage.

You hate broccoli and cabbage? Who doesn't? If staying in shape were easy, everyone would look like Sigourney Weaver. The Nobel Prize awaits the scientist who finds that Mallomars are the perfect food.

Does all this mean that your next dinner party should be entirely salad bar? No, fish is also a good antioxidant, and garlic is too. Whatever you eat, just don't eat too much of it, and between meals, keep moving. Like the engine of your car, the human body is a machine that will break down if you don't keep it in condition. The last thing you want is a valve job.

In Georgia, which is in the south of the former Soviet Union, many people live to be one hundred or more, climbing mountains, eating sour cheese, and doing backbreaking work all day. They sleep with sheep from time to time, but it's always in the clean fresh air, which keeps both species healthy.

In that remarkable place, Mirzhan Movlamov, who is now 121, conceived a son when he was eighty. From his first marriage, Mirzhan also has an eighty-four-year-old grandson, who is probably the first octogenarian grandchild of a living grandfather in all of human history.

Ever since I read about the world's most extended families and what longevity can be, I've had Georgia on my mind. Dr. Walter M. Bortz II also had those Georgians on his mind when, in *We Live Too Short and Die Too Young,* he said, "The millions of Americans who die in their sixties and seventies do so prematurely. Your sixties and seventies should be middle age."

Wouldn't it be nice to mark your seventieth birthday with a midlife crisis?

In our own country, at Minnesota's Sisters of Notre Dame convent, there are nuns who spend all their days being mentally and physically active. As a result of this activity, several are over ninety and a few are one hundred—and none show the memory loss or general decline that many such super-seniors develop. Notre Dame wins again.

However, we all are winners: As they approach the millennium, scientists are making truly dazzling achievements in the world of medicine:

- Hips are routinely being replaced. (What a wonder to be able to relocate part of your hips to a more alluring spot!)

- Lasers are routinely restoring damaged eyes. In fact, there is now a surgical procedure that actually can correct myopia.

- There are now drugs that dissolve blood clots.

- There is a new vaccine for Lyme disease and a new drug for Crohn's disease.

- Lasers are removing age spots.

- Researchers have found the gene that triggers hair loss, so gene therapy to prevent baldness may soon be at hand.

- There is a new breast-augmentation procedure that uses a woman's own implanted tissue.

- There is Viagra.

- There is the woman who last year gave birth at sixty-three.

- A cure for certain previously incurable cancers is now visible on the horizon. A new anticancer drug called AG 33–40 shows great promise.

- Last November, it was revealed that research scientists have actually discovered how to regenerate the cells of certain human organs. A breakthrough as miraculous as that makes it particularly hard to be a pessimist.

SEVEN

A Roll in the Hay Keeps the Doctor Away

While extolling the value of exercise, I didn't mention the oldest and happiest workout: the erotic aerobics that all of us have always known how to perform, the passionate push-ups that no one learns from a video.

"Oh," you are saying, "you probably mean sex."

You're ready for *Jeopardy*.

"But when we get older," you are now saying, "sex is just another treadmill. And for the older man ... well, for him the treadmill eventually stops."

You're *not* ready for *Jeopardy*; in fact, you're as wrong as your mother was when she told you sex was a chore that women had to perform; when the time came, you had to lie back and close your eyes and pretend you were having an operation. Just because a man peaks sexually at nineteen, he isn't off the slope at sixty-nine.

"It's a myth that sex is among the first biological functions to fall prey to the aging process," said the late Dr. Helen Singer Kaplan, who at the time was director of the Human Sexuality Program at New York Hospital—Cornell Medical Center. "Seventy percent of healthy seventy-year-olds have sex at least once a week."

And this is a *pre*-Viagra statistic, so don't be one of those people who say, "Oh, food has taken the place of sex in my house. I put a mirror over my kitchen table."

Just last summer, a survey of 758 women and 534 men, age sixty or over, conducted by the National Council on Aging, revealed that 74 percent of the men and 70 percent of the women were as satisfied or even more satisfied with their sex lives than they had been in their forties.

So revel in the thought that, in today's world, a rise in the stock market is not the only rise that triggers the smiles on our older faces. In fact, many psychologists say that women are increasingly allowing themselves to be sexual as they age.

"At fifty-four," says Lauren Hutton, "sex is still the most fun I have."

One of my sixty-year-old friends, an Emmy Award–winning writer, still has the sex life she had as a girl of thirty. And it's her younger partner who looks slightly tired the morning after. Octogenarian Lena Horne put it best when she said, "Honey, sex doesn't stop until you're in the grave."

Although I've taken no personal surveys, I somehow always knew that sex didn't stop when Medicare started. It ain't over till the fat lady sings. And the fat lady, if she's smart, will keep her mouth shut and lose some weight and maybe some gentleman will start singing to her.

What's really great to know is that you can

still have a real romance, a real love affair, at *any* age. The other great thing to know is that, once you've had something with somebody, the chemistry will always be there! When you look at your childhood sweetheart later in life and he looks back at you, the spark still burns. And it's a glow you will never lose.

I have always been angered by the patronizing attitude that many people have about the sexual potential of older people.

"Oh, look at those two old people together. Aren't they *cute*? Nothing is happening, of course. They probably don't even remember which of them is the male and which is the female. Just like in those old MGM musicals. While the leading man and lady kissed passionately, the camera moved to an older couple, holding hands and grinning like idiots, with their heads bobbing. Then he'd give her a big kiss on the cheek and she'd giggle 'Oh Papa!'. . . 'Oh Mama!'"

Oh bullshit!

Every one of my friends who liked sex in her youth continues to like it no matter *what* her age. I know one woman of ninety-two who had three different partners in *one weekend,* none of whom needed hip replacement—until maybe when she was through with them. Although she can't be called typical, nonagenarian sex is *not* an erogenous fluke. Romance is just as passionate, just as wrenching, just as frequent, and just as wonderful at fifty, seventy, and even ninety as it was in your teenage years. In fact, it's probably better. How many men of seventy-five spend twenty minutes trying to remove your bra? Moreover, they know you have reached an age when your diaphragm has been bronzed.

As further proof that sexuality endures for a lifetime, let me tell you about the mother of my friend Sue, who has been married four times. When I asked Sue at what age her mother became a serial bride, she said, "When she was fifty-three, when my father died." She marries and gets divorced, or the guy dies. Right now, she's dating again, and sometimes when Sue calls late at night to say, "Hello, how are you?" her mother whispers, "I can't talk now; somebody's here."

Yes, of course there can be impotence,

caused by age or other things. Now, however, we have Viagra, and even children know that Viagra is not a Spanish chanteuse. This small blue pill already has been proven to cure up to 80 percent of impotent men. If a man is with a woman and he feels that things are looking promising, he pops a Viagra, and one hour later he is ready for the earth to move, or at least a scatter rug.

No longer need a man believe the misinformation of the youth culture and feel he is sexually doomed at sixty. Even though each Viagra pill costs about ten dollars and is sometimes not covered by insurance, the pill has already caused a second sexual revolution in America. And millions of the revolutionaries are *your* age or younger!

Not long ago, I read that the Pentagon plans to supply Viagra to American troops at an estimated annual cost of fifty million dollars, a sum that otherwise might be spent on two new Marine Corps Harrier jets or forty-five Tomahawk cruise missiles. At *last* the Pentagon has its priorities right!

And there is now talk that Viagra may even

be of help to women, and not just the ballsy
ones. I don't understand how a pill that
causes erections, that increases blood flow to
the penis, could do much for a woman, but
doctors are asking: When women complain
about a lack of sexual desire, a lack of
arousal, or a lack of lubrication, are they
really suffering from a lack of blood flow to
their clitoris or vagina? Surveys have found
that as many as 50 percent of mature women
say that at one time or another they have lost
interest in sex or have had difficulty being
aroused. Could the male potency pill do for
them what Leonardo DiCaprio does for their
daughters?

While Viagra may or may not work for
women, three different drug companies are
now testing what they call a miraculous new
drug to let women achieve multiple orgasms.
Pfizer, Zonager, and Abbott Laboratories have
been using human guinea pigs to test chemicals that adjust blood flow and stimulate parts
of the brain that control sex. (I usually keep
my brain out of it.) The results of the trials
among five hundred women, five hundred

happy women, showed that more than 50 percent of them had more orgasms than usual during sex—and those pills may be on the market within two years.

Imagine: *He* takes Viagra, *she* takes the orgasm pill, and Houston, we have liftoff!

Sex, of course, must be embraced (and that is certainly the fitting word) as healthful exercise as well as fun. Last year, the *British Medical Journal* published a study that found that men between forty-five and fifty-nine who have regular sex are generally healthier than men who don't.

"What do the *British* know about sex?" you are asking.

They know this: A four-year study of almost a thousand men in Wales revealed that the mortality rate in the group that had the most sex was less than half of that of the others.

All right, that's men, but what about women? Is sex, in those deathless postcoital words, good for *you?*

You can't imagine how good!

"Steady, once-a-week monogamous sex with a man provides wonderful benefits for a woman's physiology and reproductive health," says Dr. Winnifred Cutler, founder of the Athena Institute for Women's Wellness in Chester Springs, Pennsylvania.

After a decade of research, Dr. Cutler found that weekly sex produces estrogen levels *twice* as high as those in women who have sex annually; and high estrogen levels produce many health benefits, such as more regular menstrual periods, greater fertility, increased vaginal lubrication, better resistance to stress, clearer skin, increased tolerance to pain, improved circulation, stronger bones, memory enhancement, fewer menopausal hot flashes, tooth and gum maintenance, and—because estrogen lowers dangerous cholesterol—a reduced risk of heart disease.

Yes, a roll in the hay keeps the doctor away—unless he happens to be in the hay with you.

"Making love may be the only form of exercise for some people," says one of the authors of Dr. Cutler's study, Professor George Davey Smith of Bristol University. "Telling them to do more of something they enjoy is beneficial."

According to *Men's Health,* sex three times a week burns about seventy-five-hundred calories a year and is the equivalent of jogging seventy-five miles. Yes, I know: Having sex with some of the men you've known has been as much fun as jogging seventy-five miles, but healthful exercise isn't always fun.

And, in addition to its value as aerobic exercise, sex also gives you the benefits of resistance training. No, I'm not talking about fighting him off: I'm talking about what doctors call the contraction of the muscles during arousal and orgasm.

The next time a man says, "Was it good for you?" you might reply, "Yes, especially in the abs."

Just as sex for a woman increases the level of estrogen, not only protecting her heart but also protecting against bone loss, for a man any kind of physical exercise increases testosterone, which contributes to bone and muscle development.

I realize now that all those men who kept jumping on top of models when they were young were merely trying to stay healthy.

Those girls can be considered their cardiovascular cuties.

So now you know that sex for older men and women promotes health and is not the erotic equivalent of Halley's comet. Now you know that there is regular sex at every age, but since you're a grown-up woman, keep the details to yourself. I don't want to hear how great Harry is in bed once you take him out of the walker.

I come from the generation that felt that what went on behind the bedroom door was to be discussed only by the two people inside. There is something distasteful and slightly pathetic about older people boasting of their sexual exploits to their friends. I remember when my father remarried at the age of seventy-eight. One day his new wife came to me and told me about their wedding night, the last thing in the world I wanted to hear. I said to her, "I'm glad my dad's got you, it's wonderful that something is happening, but I don't want to know the details." Like almost everyone I know, I have never been able to imagine my parents having sex.

In fact, I've always hoped that I had been launched some other way, in a petri dish perhaps.

Nature is truly wondrous, for recently older men have begun to look good to me. I remember when I would look at a man of sixty and make a rude noise. Now, however, I look and say, "Isn't he good-looking!"

Maybe it's because your eyes are failing, but one great thing about getting older is that the older men suddenly look attractive to you. And the second great thing is that you are still attractive to them. Ain't Mother Nature one smart lady!

However, what about the older woman who wants to look in the opposite direction and chronologically date down? In a society where anything goes today, where our shining goal seems to be shamelessness, is there anything wrong with getting involved with a younger man?

Not to Ursula Andress, who says, "I tell my conservative women friends who bother me about my youthful lover to go get themselves one of their own."

Not to Aretha Franklin, who says, "You know the best way to get the weight off? Not walking or jogging three miles a day. The best way is young men."

And not to Brigitte Bardot, who says, "I have always adored beautiful young men. Just because I grow older, my taste doesn't change. So if I can still have them, why not?"

Are there no *rules* about taking a younger lover? Yes, he should be finished with high school. I don't know what else; in fact, I no longer know what's right and wrong. No, that's not true: If it makes you happy, then it's right, presuming that what makes you happy isn't hurting other people or tunneling into banks. To me, morality simply means that whatever happens behind closed doors is fine, as long as it gives happiness to the people behind those doors and no pain to anyone else. I agree with the Victorians who believed that people could do anything they wanted to as long as they didn't do it in the streets and frighten the horses.

And so, when my friend Marylou Whitney got married at seventy-one to John Henrickson, who was thirty-two, I felt she should have been applauded. Marylou has been happy with John, with whom she rides, skis, and even participates in dogsled races. They are both attractive, active, and ebullient people; and when I see them together, I never see John as a swinging male nurse; I see him as an adoring partner. Marylou, in fact, constantly exercises not only her body but also the muscle of her mind by doing the *New York Times* crossword puzzle every day.

Moreover, I know two or three other women who are happily married to men from different decades, but all these couples have found themselves in the same time zones. My friend Hester has a husband who is younger than her son, and they have been happily married for nineteen years.

Hester had been married twice to slightly older men and neither marriage worked out. And then one day she told me, "I've met someone who's twenty years younger and we're getting married!"

I couldn't believe it: She was forty-one, he was twenty-one, and when they embraced, it looked like they were breaking some law. The first time I waited in a restaurant to meet him, I prayed he wouldn't come in wearing a beanie with a propeller. Well, as I said, they now have been married for nineteen years and they're as happy as any couple I know.

Last year, my forty-nine-year-old makeup artist began dating a man of twenty-nine. Did she feel as though she had adopted him?

"No," she told me, "I feel great. The only trouble is he is starting to get middle-age spread!"

The happy and rather amazing truth is that, in time, the two of them will both seem about forty; May and December often come together and blend into a common August, for I have seen a remarkable thing happen to these couples: The men grow more mature and the women more playful. Moreover, their contemporaries also mix well; the meaning of the word "contemporary" no longer is just chronological.

But what happens, you ask, if the women grow more mature and the men more playful?

Then you won't be seeing a salute to them in *Modern Bride.*

However, I have learned another encouraging truth: These seeming mismatches are often quite happy because an older woman offers a young man certain things that a younger woman doesn't, such as worldliness, competence, deep adoration, sexual expertise, and probably more money. Also, she won't keep saying "like," which women generally drop after thirty.

It is wonderful that women now have the option to date down, an option that men have always enjoyed, for, as a woman grows older and gets more specific about what she wants and *doesn't* want, she finds fewer and fewer candidates to be her Wonder Man. In high school you fell in love with every boy in your class, except perhaps the one whose fly was never closed. But when you reach forty-five and your flaw detector is finely calibrated, a good candidate seems to be coming along as often as an honest President. And so younger men are welcome additions to your player roster—*if* you keep yourself current enough so they will want to play with you.

Keeping yourself current is a matter of renovating your nature. By the time you're forty-five, you are molded into someone whose opinions and values are pretty set. Your skin may be getting loose, but your mind is tight and not easily tailored to another person. In fact, you might even be a Republican, which is never an aid to good sex. And you also are a study in self-consciousness, wondering if each new man you meet is thinking:

She has more lines than AMTRAK ... I think she weighs more than I do ... Why isn't she married? ... Or has she tried that a few times? ... Does she have any money?

What you've got to do is give yourself a mental makeover. Air out your mind and let in new ideas. Know who Quentin Tarantino and Mike Piazza are. And don't let yourself be heard saying that there hasn't been a good movie since *Gone With the Wind.*

Once you have renovated your mind, the next appealing younger man you meet is sure to find you interesting, even though *he* may think that your mention of Renoir is a reference to the goalie for the Canadiens. Yes, the older woman has to realize that she must pull out all the stops to meet a man of any age because the social scene has changed so dramatically. People no longer meet people of the other sex at square dances, malt shops, and church socials; now they meet at health clubs, Starbucks, and Barnes & Noble. And if you can't find a guy at Barnes & Noble, at least you'll find books on how to meet him. One of those books may tell you to just keep hanging around the store.

People are also meeting each other in ways I can only describe as good grief: I have heard of women who read the obituaries of other women and then find ways to express their sympathy to the widower in person.

"I'm terribly sorry about your wife. Let me stay here and rub your back while you mourn."

And I have heard of women in small communities who make delicious casseroles for men who have recently lost their wives, casseroles in which the most conspicuous ingredient is the name and phone number taped to the dish. Trying to bake their way into bridal gowns, these women leave the casseroles at the widowers' doors, and then the women hope they won't be capturing the heart of some lonely beagle.

But actually, what is so bad about these tactics? If you're an older woman and don't like being alone, then *do* something about it the way the casserole cuties do. As the song says, "What good is sitting alone in your room?" Life may not be a cabaret—it's more like a cafeteria—but you have to keep plunging into it and trying to serve yourself. From time to time, women tell me about the joy of living alone, and I think they almost believe it; but I believe that, to coin a phrase, people who need people are the luckiest people in the world.

So have a dinner party or go to a movie with friends or donate blood or tour a museum or get your M.A. or go to a hospital and volunteer to read to children. Now that my daughter is married, she doesn't ask me to read to her very much, so I have a choice: I can sit alone in my empty nest, thinking of new numbers for my age, or I can go out and see everything from a new restaurant to an old flea market.

Believe me, I know it's hard to visit an art exhibit or theater alone, but you have to try. I've been there alone, the only woman getting her coat on a long checkroom line of men, but one time, a man next to me asked me if I was single, for he had a brother who . . . And so, in the deathless words of that great philosopher Fats Waller, "One never knows, do one?" Or, as that Waller contemporary, my mother, used to say, "Go. Maybe you'll meet someone."

Kitty Carlisle Hart tells the story of a night when she was sitting home alone, feeling sorry for herself. Her mother called and said, "Are you going to that big theatrical party?"

"I was invited," said Kitty, "but I really don't feel like going alone."

"Kitty, go," her mother commanded.

And so Kitty went to the party and met the man she married, Moss Hart.

I am lucky enough to have a man in my life right now, but if I had a void in that particular department, I would try to put myself into some male-dominated activity, some part of life where I would meet great numbers of men. Not necessarily a job in a sperm bank, but what about a rock-climbing club? Or I would take a course in world policy or volunteer at a hospital. Yvette Mimieux, the movie star, met her husband at an environmental group.

Helena Hacker Rosenberg, author of *How to Get Married After 35,* echoes my advice by saying, "You have to get out and change your social landscape. You have to shake up your routine by going to new places and doing new things. Find a new routine for every day, whether it's a new place for your morning coffee or a visit to a new art gallery or something as simple as changing your route for walking to work."

French journalist Dominique Aury felt at forty-something, "I wasn't young, I wasn't pretty, so it was necessary to find other weapons." And so, taking the pseudonym Pauline Réage, she wrote the sexually explicit *Story of O* specifically to attract a man. Not only did it work but it changed her entire life.

"The only thing you have to fear is change itself," says Helena Rosenberg, who met and married her own husband when she was in her forties. "The only thing scarier than actually making changes in my life—going to new places, avoiding the types of people who tended to lead to dead-end relationships—was the thought that I might end up alone."

Just as you cannot be timid about scouting new hunting grounds, you cannot be timid with people either. It is said that faint heart never won fair lady, and when the lady is doing the pursuing, a shy try never gets the guy. So don't be ashamed to keep asking your friends, "Who do you know?" Or, if you want to find a higher class of man, ask it grammatically: "*Whom* do you know?"

Yes, of *course* it can sometimes be hard for a woman in her middle years to meet a new man because men in *their* middle years often prefer younger women.

One woman in her late forties told me, "The only men who take me out for a whirl are cabdrivers."

This woman, of course, should tell her cab-drivers to take her to bookstores, clubs, and museums.

I know, I know: Half the men you meet belong in museums. Well, you simply have to keep circulating. After her divorce, a woman I know asked a friend, "How do you meet men?"

"Entertain," the friend replied.

"You mean in the bedroom?" said the divorcée.

"No, in your *dining* room. Keep inviting people to your home and they'll keep inviting you back."

What about the Internet? There are *150 million* copies of Windows 95 now in use! And did you know that almost 20 percent of the Americans now online are over fifty? And many of them aren't looking for tax shelters, plumbers, or asteroids. An increasingly popular way to meet the opposite sex today is in chat rooms on the Internet, another good reason to learn to use a personal computer.

Moreover, the Internet is 70 percent men, so the odds are definitely in a woman's favor that she can find a guy online.

Of course, a woman in pursuit can also find a guy on parole, so be careful about what you reveal in cyberspace and where you meet in person.

While searching for Mr. Right, whether online at a computer terminal or on line at a fish store, consider the value of a pet as matchmaker. Not only is a pet a wonderful companion who makes you get up and go out, but once you are out walking Bowser, you'll meet his pals and their walkers too. I know at least four two-legged couples who've been brought together by four-footed friendships forged at the lower end of a leash.

Should you try to meet a man by running a personal ad in a newspaper or magazine or on a supermarket wall? In this Age of No Shame, should you offer yourself to the public with a few coolly objective words?

Gorgeous, witty, athletic, sensuous, sensitive, soulful, athletic, noble, creative, compassionate, Mensa-bound lay princess of indeterminate age would like to begin a fabulous adventure with the smart, hip, fiftyish prince of a plastic surgeon who has been dreaming of her while lifting inferior faces. I'm a Michelle Pfeiffer look-alike, I love to walk on the beach where you vacation a few times a year, I'm whatever religion you'd like me to be, and I'm better in bed than your nurse. Send photo, but I like your face already.

Such an ad would capture you nicely, of course, but the problem is, it may bring you responses from princes whose photos are in the post office.

A friend of mine once tried to meet men through a video dating service, where both sexes leave tapes and then the service calls you in to screen a few that seem likely to produce a good match.

"It didn't turn out to be the greatest idea," she told me. "The guy I liked best had said he was single with no children, but when I called him, a babysitter answered. Either the guy was married or he was living with a babysitter."

Going beyond video is a new computerized

dating service called Relationship Line, which lets subscribers hear dozens of telephonic messages from people with different backgrounds. To get an idea of what is out there for a single woman in her middle years, I picked up the phone one day, called Relationship Line, and got a free introductory offer: I listened to some messages from men between fifty and sixty, each of whom revealed that he had just dropped down from Mount Olympus.

"But I can't help falling in love with you," sang one male voice with all the appeal of a telemarketer. "*Hi,* this is Alan. I'm handsome, slim, witty, creative, athletic, boyish, compassionate, and tall."

Well, he probably was named Alan.

"And I'm seeking a very bright, attractive, cultured, funny woman with a little girl inside."

Alan was certainly wise to request the mind of a little girl, for only a six-year-old could have fallen for such an oily ego.

Oily ego was the dominant tone of these messages, most of which were as bewitching as a crank call.

"Let's see if our quirks are compatible," said another man. "I'd like you to be good-looking and slim. And a natural redhead is a big plus."

To counterbalance Mr. Big Minus, a man with sterling values, "I'm industrious, hard-working, and loyal," said another, who sounded like a cocker spaniel.

"I'm looking for a bright, easygoing, well-built woman in her fifties," said another. "Someone buxom and zaftig because zaftig appeals to me. In fact, I'm zaftig myself."

A man with nice boobs?

However, in spite of this circus parade, if you approach this kind of lottery with a sense of humor and a tight budget, it might be worth a fling or two. Relationship Line costs fifty dollars for three months. Maybe you'll find a zaftig man who runs deeper than his flab. One of my friends did. She and her new architect husband are currently building their dream house.

A word of caution: Just as on the Internet, when you meet a man through any of these services, you must be *careful* about not revealing your name and address right away—because you never *know*. Arrange to meet him not at your house but at a neutral place. And go slowly. Anyone can say anything he wants to on the Relationship Line; no one checks the veracity.

Another reason to be careful when bringing a new person into your life is a monetary one: When you reach a certain age, your earning capacity starts to decline, even if your *yearning* capacity is still going strong. I know it's not romantic to have a lawyer in bed with you and Mr. Beloved. I know a prenuptial agreement doesn't go with moonlight. But if you're going to marry the guy, you've got to protect yourself financially against the unhappy ending that comes to half the marriages in America.

Of course, that statistic also means that half the marriages *succeed*, but again, you can never be too careful.

In all your reaching out to new people, don't let fear of the unknown prevent you from "dating down" if the guy rings your bells. Don't turn up your nose at the United Parcel man; not every husband has to be a lawyer or doctor.

Those UPS guys do look cute in their brown shorts, especially if they have good legs. And if you want even *more* romance, mail carriers also wear pith helmets.

It doesn't cost much to have a cup of coffee with *any* man, whether he's delivering your mail or selling you a car or even working in your office. There used to be a rule about not getting involved with someone in your office, but that rule has now gone the way of the slide rule. A *New York* magazine survey last year revealed that, of the 3 million single people in New York, 39 percent said that they had had sex with a coworker, a figure appropriate for the time of Bill Clinton.

We used to find our mates on blind dates or at parties or in the community, but now the workplace has taken over as *the* place to meet. These days, the water cooler should be playing "Three Coins in the Fountain."

Last Valentine's Day, a New York TV station reported the results of another survey in which 40 percent of the professional people polled said they had dated a coworker and 70 percent said the relationship had worked out well. For the other 30 percent . . . well, they'd been wanting a reason to polish up their résumés.

You might even find a man at a high school or college class reunion, so go to as many as you can, whether they are yours or not, if you remember the men in that class as being attractive. But also be prepared: Almost all the men will be married, of course, so you have to subtly find out which ones are not. A good way to start is to check their left hand for a ring, and then approach them.

SHE: Ron Wren? It's Jean McDermott. I'm a friend of your wife.

HE: Jean McDermott? Why . . . you look *terrific*! Are you *sure* you're Class of '56?

SHE: Oh, '56, '66—I was never good with figures.

HE: Except your own.

SHE: That's sweet. I try to work out. A little
     biathlon now and then.

HE: Is your husband here?

SHE: I'm single. Is your wife here?

HE: (looking hard at her) I hope so.

At a reunion, a party, or a fire sale, absolutely nothing is more important than staying active, involved, and *current*. You have to be dated only if you're cream cheese.

Things to Remember When You're in a Hospital

- Never say you threw out your back while bending for your Social Security check. Say it happened while starring in a porno film.

- If you are there for a triple bypass, don't use the short-term parking.

- If you still have a good body, wear your hospital gown backward.

- At bedtime, don't look for a chocolate on your pillow.

- Never leave in the middle of your surgery for a sale at Bloomingdale's.

- Have meaningful conversations with your nurse. Ask her, "What young movie stars have been through this dump on their way to rehab?"

- Don't tell Sven the orderly that you want to introduce him to your cousin, who is gay as a goose.

EIGHT

No Fool's Gold for Your Golden Years

"Gee, I can't wait till I can retire and just do *nothing* all day!" Americans have been saying for years. "Won't it be *wonderful* to just lie around and have absolutely nothing to do!"

The answer is: Absolutely not. In fact, rather than just lying around, you'll probably be going downhill fast. Any good doctor will tell you that being a slug is wonderful only if you live under a rock. And while traveling all over this country to talk to women about bettering their lives, I have learned that, for too many people, a retirement community often has all the appeal of a minimum security prison with palms.

I have always liked Bob Hope's line. When asked if he was going to retire, Bob replied, "To what?" However, he finally did slow down a bit in his mid-nineties, when he said, "I don't generally feel anything until noon. Then it's time for my nap."

Yes, *my* advice to anyone even toying with the idea of retirement is one word: Don't. I truly believe it is better to expire than to retire.

In the words of Helen Hayes, that indefatigable trouper of the stage, "If you rest, you rust."

To put it more lyrically by paraphrasing a line from Cole Porter: Doing nothing is my idea of nothing to do, a basic truth that shocks too many older people after they have moved to a place with no children, pets, or change of seasons, after they have sold their homes and gone south to stare at the sprinklers, play shuffleboard, and eat dinner at five o'clock.

The paradise of retirement is possibly the

most dangerous myth in America today. What could be dumber than glorifying stagnation?

Ever since a builder named Del Webb invented the leisure village at Sun City, Arizona, more than forty years ago, leisure villages have been replacing real life all over the South and West. And each of them should carry a warning from the Surgeon General: *Age segregation, endless sunshine, and inactivity are hazardous to both physical and mental health.*

As you now know, the most important message I have for you is: *Stay in the arena and stay active and purposeful there with all kinds of people. That* will make you happy, but to me happiness feels elusive for people trapped in a world of sunny sterility. And once you drop out of the arena, it's hard to *get back in.*

Many people, of course, do manage to find a certain contentment when living in retirement communities, or "golden ghettos," as Margaret Mead called them, but they are living in low gear; they are living half-lives. And the stories told by many of their neighbors are not testimonials to Century Village.

If a person is content doing nothing in endless sunshine, why have I heard tales like these?

In one leisure village near Miami, there was almost a fistfight in the clubhouse over whether the grass should be cut in the morning or the evening. Mowing time, not weapons of mass destruction, was the issue to start a war.

In another Florida paradise, people almost came to blows over whether the soft drink machines in the clubhouse should be dispensing Pepsi or Coke. People living their golden years? If such petty matters can upset them, think how empty their lives must be!

The builders of retirement villages have been promoting two great lies: that older people are happiest in a place where every day is Sunday, and that older people are happiest when surrounded only by people their own age.

When giving talks in the Southwest, I happened to pass through Sun City, Arizona, and it depressed me enormously. One woman there told me that she actually went to Phoenix every weekend just to see children ice skating. She needed a youth fix. And another woman there told me, "I never knew how much I could miss hearing a baby cry," a line sadder than some I have heard from TV executives.

"I sold my whole library when I left New Jersey," said a third, "and I really miss those books. Now Sam and I just sit here and play cards and wait for the grandchildren to visit."

"Well, at least it's fun when the kids come," I told her.

"No, it isn't. You see, I have to sneak the kids in because they're sort of against the rules."

"I guess when you're two feet tall, it's hard to lie about your age," I said. "Do the kids really mind swimming at midnight?"

Yes, racial segregation is long gone in America, but age segregation is growing, and some of it is beyond belief.

One Florida leisure village actually evicted the younger wife of a resident because she'd become pregnant; the fear of children was that idiotic. Another resident, however, was allowed to keep a pet monkey, undoubtedly because the monkey didn't act immature.

At Leisure World of Laguna Beach, I asked a woman in her sixties if she missed having young people around.

"Absolutely not," she replied. "Young people can be so obnoxious."

No one over thirty, of course, is ever obnoxious.

The point is simply that the only healthful life, the only *worthwhile* life, is not just an active and purposeful one but an *intergenerational* one too. And you'll stay mentally young if you not only mix with younger people but understand them without being judgmental.

Never let yourself say something like, "But the kids don't dress up anymore." Your mother felt the same way about you when she used to tell you, "Wear your gloves." And I confess to having asked my daughter Melissa more than once, "Where are your stockings?" To which she probably wanted to reply, "*In your hat.*" I am repelled by kids who wear their caps backward, but I never suggest a different position because I remember how repelled my mother was by the dirty white buck shoes of my dates.

"The younger generation is noisy, arrogant, and rude. It has no respect for its elders."

You know who said that? No, not Jerry Falwell. Aristotle said it. So you see, things started going downhill a few years ago.

Many older people are lucky enough to know the value of purposeful and intergenerational activity, so they resist the siren song of the Sun Belt that keeps tempting them to cut their ties with real life. On a PBS broadcast about retirement last year, a man of sixty from Boston, who had rejected going to one of Florida's huge Century Villages, said, "Would I want to be surrounded by thirteen thousand people all the *same age*? I'd feel cut off from the real noises of life."

I love those noises and I dread ever having to wear earplugs. One evening a few years ago, I went to a dinner party for a legendary actress. All the people there were her contemporaries: All were in their late seventies, except for the ones in their eighties. Sitting with those people, I felt as though an ambulance were about to arrive. I looked around the table, wondering if anyone knew CPR, and I said to myself, *This is wrong.* Didn't she have any younger friends except me? Well, I have a *lot* of younger friends and I plan to keep it that way. In fact, it keeps getting easier.

At any age, you have to do more than just kill time or time will quickly kill you. You have to stay in action. Watching TV while waiting for your husband to finish playing golf doesn't count.

"My husband plays golf three or four hours every day," one Florida woman told me, "but I don't, so it leaves me kind of bored. How much bridge can I play?"

As we talked, I learned that both she and her husband often missed the richness of the life of the northern community where they had grown up. They missed their family ties, their old friends, and the intergenerational mix. Other people in her leisure village said the same thing.

"I missed seeing the seasons change," one woman told me.

How blue you can be when you never see the leaves turn red! And how bored you can be when every day is Sunday. We all need Monday mornings and Thursday nights in winter, spring, and fall to keep our minds alive. Doctors have told me that a constant change of season is definitely better for your mind and your body than endless stifling heat. (There was a lot of discontent on Devil's Island.) In fact, doctors have said that cold is actually more healthful than heat.

What so many of these segregated seniors miss even more than their old support systems is a sense of *purpose,* which is essential at *every* age. You've *got* to have a better reason to get up in the morning than to plan your lunch.

People who make the mistake of retiring to live only for pleasure usually discover the sad truth of something Fred Astaire said in a film called *The Pleasure of His Company:*

"The life of nothing but pleasure demands a concentration and discipline far beyond the capacities of most people. It's a talent that very few have."

In short, you can't really have fun if fun is all you have.

A New York newspaper reporter named Jane Glenn Haas recently asked her uncle, who has spent twenty-eight years not working, "How has retirement been for you?"

"Boring," he replied. "After the first ten years of playing golf, it's all been downhill."

Another regretful retiree told Jane, "I'd rather be working. If I had it all to do over again, I'd look for a position to at least stay active. I miss not being involved with the community."

And the retired father of a friend of mine has this advice for new arrivals to his Sunny Acres Garden of Eden: "Never read the newspaper first thing in the morning because then you'll have nothing to do the rest of the day."

As the kids like to say: "Get a life." And a life qualifies as one only if it gives you that reason to get up in the morning. Playing golf, gin rummy, or bingo all day with only people your own age just doesn't qualify as an acceptable lure for leaving bed. Shakespeare, who decided not to put his mother in a condo at Avon Estates, said it nicely in *Henry IV*:

> **If all the year were playing holidays,**
> **To sport would be as tedious as to work.**

Even Jackie Kennedy Onassis learned the truth of these lines when, at the age of forty-five, she suddenly found that she was bored, with little to talk about, and then one of her friends suggested that she go to work.

Now, going to work might seem foolish for someone who had more money than the government of Guatemala, but counting your money can't get you through the day, unless you work at the mint. And so Jackie got a job as a book editor for a salary that was probably less than what she was paying her cook.

A good friend of mine has a grandson named Max, who was exactly one and a half when he revealed a stunning bit of wisdom. My friend and Max were playing together when Max suddenly smiled and said, "Happy." And a moment later, he said,

"Busy." Here was a toddler who already knew that there is a direct connection between happy and busy. Max never would have said, "Happy. Killing time." Or, "Happy. Involved in another day of pointless passive pleasure."

In spite of his genius, Thomas Jefferson made one mistake in the Declaration of Independence: He talked about "the pursuit of happiness." But you cannot *pursue* happiness; you cannot chase an abstraction. Happiness is a *by-product* of being busily involved in rewarding activity. A person who is truly happy, like a scientist hunting for the best estrogen, never thinks about "happiness." A one-year-old can tell you that.

"Okay," you're saying, "then what should an older person *do* if he or she no longer has work?"

The answer is: Don't leave the mainstream of real life. Stay there and fight to get back in if you've been pushed out. And believe me, getting pushed out because of age happens to the best of us. You already know about Isabella Rossellini and Joan Lunden being tossed out. Well, Jane Seymour was pushed out at CBS, and Helen Gurley Brown was replaced after thirty-two years of running *Cosmopolitan,* and less than two years later, Ruth Whitney was pushed out of her editor's chair at *Glamour* by the same Boomer Babe who had replaced Helen.

If, like those ladies, you're forced to leave your day job, you first must take a deep breath and say to yourself, "This is life. Even though it's unfair and horrible, there is nothing I can do about it, so I'm moving forward and I'm never looking back. I'm going through that door and forward on the other side."

And then go out and look for paid work. I say "paid" because money in return for your services makes you feel validated and valued as an asset in the workplace; earned money gives you worth. There is, of course, nothing wrong with volunteering; in fact, as I've said, there is everything *right* with it. Everyone should, in fact, pay her dues by doing good work for free, but do it in your leisure hours.

In your job search, try not to stray far from the limb from which you were pushed. Were you an airline pilot? Then try to become a

flight trainer. Were you a teacher? Then try
to give private lessons. A hooker? Then turn
a real trick and become a madam.

If you can't find a job in your old line of
work, then be prepared to do the really hard
work of reinventing yourself by learning new
skills. Take computer lessons, learn a language, do anything you have to do to make
yourself a valuable new asset in the workplace.

Roddy McDowall kept reinventing himself
in the attempt to shake off his image as a
child actor, an image that clung to him in the
minds of many fossils still stuck in the past.
Even as he breathed his last at the age of seventy, Roddy said, "My whole life I've been trying to prove I'm not yesterday." And how he
succeeded!

As has Joanne Woodward. About a decade
ago, when the only work she could find was
playing old ladies in bathrobes (Goldie Hawn
said, "There are three ages for women in
Hollywood: Babe, District Attorney, and
Driving Miss Daisy"), Joanne decided to "get a
new hairdo and look terrific and go back to

school. And even if nobody notices, I'm going to be the most self-fulfilled lady on the block." She then went on to earn a degree from Sarah Lawrence, and instead of returning to the screen, she now devotes most of her time to political and social causes.

That, more or less, is what you have to do if you've been dumped from your job and the business of finding paid work doesn't work for you. You must continue to look outward, not inward. You don't have to be Plato or even Charlie Brown to know that it's up to you to *generate* a rewardingly busy life the way Joanne Woodward did, a life in which the highlight of your day isn't *As the World Turns* or waiting for the winning lottery numbers or a letter from Ed McMahon with a new chance not to win a million dollars.

In other words, start your own world turning and *volunteer*. I got as much reward from delivering food to AIDS patients in the program called God's Love We Deliver as I got from winning an Emmy, and I plan to keep doing it until someone has to start feeding *me*.

I know a woman in New York named Molly Pickett, who is eighty-six. Almost every day for the last fifteen years, she has delivered food to—as she calls them—"older people," who are poor and too weak to leave their apartments. Moreover, Molly has a boyfriend of eighty-five named Bob, who also makes food deliveries around Manhattan—on his *bicycle*. Molly and Bob know that life at its best is *giving* and worrying about someone besides yourself.

The secret of staying young is to stay connected to life and involved in life and to keep learning new things, an approach that will hold off the depression that tends to increase as we age. And nothing is more depressing than to wake up and know that your only plan for the day is to stay alive until dinner.

The truth is, we're staying alive a lot longer than *that*, so there's more time than ever to either fill or kill. Today, when the human life span keeps increasing, it is simply insane to drop out of active life at fifty-five or sixty. And rewarding activity is one of the ways to keep that life span growing. It's not really a joke that a British sitcom set in a retirement community is called *Waiting for God.*

And so, keep moving. It's hard for old age to hit a moving target.

I'm happy to see that many of the baby boomers are already planning to be moving targets. At Florida's International University, there is now a course called "Retirement for Baby Boomers," which I wish I could have taken at college instead of geology. Perhaps the final is an essay on tanning. Perhaps for extra credit, you can go to Club Med.

And perhaps I shouldn't be flip about a change in American attitude that is profoundly wise. The course's teacher, Professor Tim Patton, says that when they reach sixty-five, baby boomers will retire *without* retiring: They will shift gears from full-time to part-time work, but they will stay mentally and physically involved in life.

Laying the groundwork for a productive future is something all of us should do, no matter what our age. In fact, it is never too early to start, even if you're only in your thirties.

When you're in your thirties and not married, it is time to decide if you want to have that child anyway. Or, if you're married, how close a race do you want to run with your biological clock? And do you want to buy a house? It is also time to make a will and to get your health insurance in order so that you won't wake up at fifty and say, "Where is this? Why don't I have that? Why didn't I buy . . . ?"

If you do not have children to mark the passage of time, it's easy not to realize that you are aging. That's a happy thing but unfortunate too because you tend to forget that, in your thirties, it's time to plan for your future.

When you're in your forties, whether married or single, and you're not happy with your career, it is time to make a change, to go for the big job. Do it now. Ten years from now, people will look at you and think you've peaked, but in your forties, you are still not fully formed professionally. And if you do have children, now is the time to prepare for the empty-nest syndrome, which will hit you hard. And so you had better be very busy or you'll feel lonely, useless, and abandoned when you're the only bird in that nest.

For women, fifty is the really bad time, when you look in the mirror and hate what you see, and you find yourself shouting at that stranger looking back at you, "Whose mother are you? Where did Ellen go?"

On the day I turned fifty, I refused to get out of bed. I just lay there all day with the covers over my head. But now that friends of mine are turning fifty and sobbing over it, I look at them and think they're crazy because, from my current vantage point, they look like teenagers. Wouldn't it be a happy bit of time travel if we had the power to look at ourselves ten years into the future? The vision would make us feel so young!

Yes, fifty is awful only till you are past it, till you realize the dreaded birthday is over, and now you can get on with your life. Moreover, you are suddenly aware of all the wonderful-looking people who are in their fifties, people like Diane Sawyer, Catherine Deneuve, Faye Dunaway, Lauren Hutton, Candice Bergen, Goldie Hawn, Susan Sarandon, Ann-Margret, and Joni Mitchell. The men look good too: Michael Douglas, George Hamilton, Martin Scorsese, and Prince Charles. And their fifties will have even more appeal when you hit sixty.

Although retirement communities are now trying to lure people as young as fifty, even some retirees are starting to realize the wisdom of endless involvement versus sunny stupor. In a PBS program called *My Retirement Dreams,* some residents of a south Florida condominium knew that they had to stay active and upbeat if they wanted to avoid being anesthetized by sunbathing, shuffleboard, and bridge. They are learning that the bridge to a healthy life has no dummy.

Many people in other countries have possessed this wisdom for centuries, people who've never read a single book. Think of that rocky region of southern Russia that I mentioned in an earlier chapter, where the goat herders routinely live to one hundred, climbing those mountains until the very end and never thinking of pension plans or senior discounts or when their great-great-grandchil-

dren will call. None of those hardy centenari-
ans ever says, "Katrina, let's leave the goats
and take a time-share on the Black Sea.
These are our golden years."

For these people, there is no Crimean
Association of Retired Persons.

To show you that I put my feet where my
mouth is, last spring I decided that my
involvement with the *new* would include a
ten-day safari with friends to the wilds of
Kenya, where, as I mentioned earlier, I lived
among the Masai. Well, it didn't take me long
to assume the missionary position: I was
praying.

Shortly after a guide had told us never to
leave our vehicle when lions were near, we
found ourselves hopelessly stuck in a marsh
in lion country. I wanted to call the AAA
(African Automobile Association), but I realized we would have to push our way out—
which meant getting out of those vehicles.
While doing so, I took comfort from one
thought: I was the runt of the group, so the
lions would eat me last. We got out, scared to
death, and indeed pushed our way back to

camp. Scared to death? Yes. Totally exhilarated? *Yes!* Even in the midst of our trouble, I was thrilled to be a part of such a glorious adventure.

Every night, we had the fun of zipping up our tents to keep out the animals that wanted to "play with us." When I suggested in an earlier chapter that you get a pet, I had in mind a single poodle, not fifty chimpanzees. The intergenerational life is fine. The inter*species* life has its limits.

One evening, I didn't zip properly and a monkey slipped in, probably to take a closer look at what his family had evolved down to. Unfortunately, I had to stop appreciating his cuteness when he swung directly above me and dropped an intestinal souvenir into my hair. You will pardon my earthy speech, but ape shit took on new meaning for me.

Yes, for much of the time in Kenya, I was nervous and edgy, but I loved every minute because I knew that life is either a glorious journey or it is nothing. Even when I found myself looking for the nonexistent hair and makeup tent, I enjoyed knowing that I was in the arena and not in a place where I would be going to the early bird dinner. In fact, if I weren't careful, the early bird dinner would be me.

I have told you not to accept limits, but of course there are times when you *do* have to accept a few little ones—for example, when you go on safari in your sixties. Because I was the oldest person in our safari, I paced myself, aware that I cannot do at sixty-five what I did at twenty-five. In fact, I'm not sure how blithely I would have done one or two things at twenty-five. In Larchmont, I didn't have much practice in getting up at dawn to look for white rhinos when the temperature was thirty-five degrees. And so I paced myself in subtle ways, always making sure that I had my medications with me, carried extra water, and tried to return an hour before the others. By nine o'clock on safari, I had assumed the missionary position.

One of the dismaying realizations triggered by my trip to Africa was how badly America treats its older people: They suffer a conspicuous shortage of respect, which can be seen when they have to suffer birthday greetings from Willard Scott. By contrast, in the Masai tribe, everyone strives to become an elder—not that anyone *there* is going in the other direction either. They may know that aging sucks, but they still strive to become elders because the elders are considered the wisest people. They set the standards and make the big decisions. They are looked up to as people of vision. In America, we look up to Leonardo DiCaprio. In Africa, the vision of someone twenty-three years old would be considered a form of blindness.

People Whom Older People Should Have the License to Kill

- Anyone who says, "You are soooo cute."

- Anyone who uses the word "spry."

- Funeral directors who take you aside at funerals and whisper, "You might just as well stay."

- Sexy, good-looking men who put their arm around you and say, "How's my girl?"

- Any man who says, as the bar is closing, "Well, I guess it's you or the bouncer. Come on, Guido."

NINE

The Kindest Cut

In a memorable moment in *The Graduate,* an adult meaningfully says to the young man, "Ben—I want to say one word to you—just one word—*plastics.*"

Well, I have just *two* words for you: *plastic surgery.*

No matter how well you exercise or how wisely you eat, no matter how fetching your clothes, hair, or home may be, no matter how active you are in the arena or in bed, that old enemy time is still going to leave lines on your face. Yes, there are people who tell you that you've earned your wrinkles, ruts, and crow's-feet, that lines make your face look lived in, and that a lived-in face is a sign of character. Well, those people lie. Lines, except Cunard, are bad. Lines simply make you look old.

During my travels around the country as a kind of floating cheerleader for spunk, I've met thousands of women who have asked me, "Should I have plastic surgery?"

And my answer is always a resounding "Yes. It will make you feel better about yourself."

Unfair but true: In spite of the graying of America, we live in a society where youth counts, where looks count, where the whole package counts. *Everyone* wants to look good, and not only in America. Throughout the ages, most of the rest of the world has felt that way too. Think of the paintings you treasure most, by artists like Raphael and Rembrandt. The beauty they capture is the beauty of youth. Mona Lisa was no more than thirty; Lancôme could have used her as its spokeswoman.

There is simply no question that, when it

comes to our faces and our bodies, age is a weapon of mass destruction. Joyce Carol Oates was wrong when she said, "Getting wrinkles is trivial." And Golda Meir also was wrong when she said, "Old age is like flying through a storm. Once you're aboard, there's nothing you can do about it."

Wrong! Wrong! Wrong! There's *everything* you can do about it. No woman today has to go and pull the shutters and sit around under a hat with a scarf around her neck. I don't care who you are or how old; you can get something done. In fact, I don't consider it an option, I consider it an obligation. It's your duty to look amazing for your age.

"But," you're asking, "can a feminist have a face-lift?"

To which my response is: Is Netanyahu Jewish? Did Al Jolson sing "Mammy"? Does Bill Gates have any money?

Letty Cottin Pogrebin, one of the founders of *Ms*. magazine (more feminist than that you cannot get), pondered the question not long ago and came up with this answer:

"Why not give myself a nip and tuck as a

midlife present? When my husband and I got tired of the cramped layout of our house, we took down a wall between two rooms and everything was transformed. Why shouldn't I do the same when it comes to *self*-improvement?"

And it doesn't have to be a *midlife* treat. I gave myself a post-teen present when I did my eyes at thirty-two. My mother and father had left me a legacy that wasn't in their will: a bag under each eye, a nicely matched set. My genes had given me more luggage than I wanted to carry, so I checked it in an operating room.

In fact, many doctors say it's wise to have plastic surgery early, because your skin will respond better and because there is less chance of people noticing that you've had anything done. They will think you look great, either because you've been taking splendid care of yourself (which you certainly have) or because you've been in Mexico for a month. The surgery will probably cost as much as a month in Mexico, but a new face is a better souvenir than an Indian blanket.

What I don't want to hear is that you can't

find the money for plastic surgery. If you can afford a trailer home, you can afford a face-lift. If you can buy a Honda, you can buy yourself surgical happiness. So forget the home and forget the car. If a Porsche pulls up driven by a woman who needs a face-lift, the picture is all wrong; the woman has made the wrong choice of where to put her money. Better to have the mileage show on your old car than to have it show on *you*!

Borrow the money if you have to; beg for it if you must. I'm not suggesting you dip into the church plate, but I'm a firm believer in giving to yourself. Charity should begin with you: with your face, your body, and any other part that shows.

I can't say, of course, how much your surgeon will charge; prices vary greatly. The challenge is to find the best one there is without sending you into Chapter 11. That may mean finding a young doctor (and he *should* be younger than you so that you can form a lifelong relationship), a doctor who perhaps is a Great One's assistant and about to break into a practice of his own.

You can also try to negotiate the fee, offer to stagger the payments, even make a barter deal—not trade ten chickens for a tummy tuck but offer some service the doctor might like. In exchange for a face-lift, a friend of mine who teaches yoga gives the wife of her plastic surgeon free weekly yoga sessions for a year. I wonder how much new face ten of my monologues might bring?

My motto is: "Anything that can be lifted should be lifted. Anything that falls should be caught. And try to catch any falling stuff before it hits the ground."

The face, of course, comes first. When you're about thirty-five, have that initial "training" lift, a prophylactic lift, some people call it, and you'll also probably want to do your eyes and the area under your eyes in the vicinity of your jawbone.

In the years since I removed the baggage from my eyes, I've gone for the Full Monty twice—the first time at forty-nine and the second at fifty-seven, for the tightening doesn't hold indefinitely. The average face-lift lasts between five and ten years. However, every two years, I return to my plastic surgeon to see if anything needs to be touched up—perhaps a tuck here, a brow lift there, perhaps nothing anywhere.

To me, plastic surgery has been a two-year tune-up that makes me feel good about myself. It's like Simonizing my body, the care of which I put ahead of my car. I can't lease a new Joan Rivers. They don't make them anymore. There was never much of a call.

"Outward appearance can indeed affect inner feelings and self-esteem," says Dr. Eugenie Brunner, an eminent plastic surgeon in Princeton, New Jersey. "It can't make you look like someone else or guarantee job success or make people like you. What it can do is improve the harmony and balance of your facial features, reverse some of the signs of aging, and help you look your best."

A balanced face has always been my dream, especially since I've never been able to achieve that with my mind. And there seem to be as many surgical ways to balance a face as there are faces in search of balancing. Consider this beginner's list:

- Cold lasers to remove wrinkles from the outer layer of the skin.

- Hot lasers to tighten the deeper layer.

- Blepharoplasty for the eyelids, upper and lower.

- Rhinoplasty for a straighter, smaller, or slimmer nose.

- Lipocontouring for the neck and jawline.

- Chin implants.

- Cheek lifts.

- Ear tack-backs to correct the Dumbo syndrome.

- Full facial lifts with CO_2 and erbium lasers.

- A la carte: You name it and a plastic surgeon will do it.

You must not *overdo* it, of course. I know one woman who has plastic surgery the way I have haircuts. In an effort to keep looking ever younger, she is headed back to the womb.

She also may be headed for trouble. There comes a point, after the fourth or fifth lift, where the skin is stretched to the breaking point. One more lift and it will split apart. However, no reputable plastic surgeon would let your skin look as though it has been through a shredder. Even Jocelyn Wildenstein's face is still connected to her ears.

"But suppose *I* come out looking like a Transylvanian experiment?" you ask.

Well, there *is* some risk, although the overwhelming odds say that you won't emerge from plastic surgery with your nose near your ear. But I believe that even a bad lift is better than no lift at all. If it's too tight, don't worry; it'll loosen and those chipmunk cheeks will fall.

However, as sportsmen like to say, sometimes even a thoroughbred stumbles, and plastic surgery is still an invasive procedure and there *is* the possibility of infection, hemorrhage, blood clot, allergic reaction, and even death. Therefore, choose your surgeon carefully; check him out before *you* check out, and then look at before and after pictures of his patients. The after pictures should look better.

Once you have chosen a surgeon, be sure to give him a realistic goal. Don't bring him a picture of Gwyneth Paltrow, unless you think he'd like it for his wall. You must be aware that plastic surgery won't turn a fifty-year-old woman into a twenty-year-old Chiclet. Instead, it will make the fifty-year-old the most beautiful fifty-year-old she can be. Plastic surgery is a kind of cosmetic miracle, but it will *not* turn you into Cindy Crawford. It will, however, make you look a little less like Broderick Crawford.

Once you have chosen your surgeon, listen to everything he says. After surgery, I always like to stay overnight in the doctor's own hospital. I find it comforting to have someone nearby say, "This is right" or "This is wrong" or "This is all covered by insurance."

You may be wondering how much discomfort is involved. Well, the recovery is less fun than a day at Disneyland, but the surgery itself doesn't hurt because you're anesthetized, either by a general or a local. And for many procedures, you're an outpatient. You do look like hell when you leave the hospital, but every day you look better and better. It's the happiest healing process.

The case for facial plastic surgery—cosmetic surgery is a better term—comes down to this: It is just so damn nice when you hit sixty to have someone say, "Don't you look wonderful!" Someone who isn't lying, that is. Every year, about a hundred thousand facelifts are done in America, 90 percent on women, 60 percent of whom are over fifty. It's the kindest cut of all.

And you don't have to resort to the scalpel or even the laser to give your face a boost. There is dermabrasion, in which fine lines are sort of sanded away, and there is also the chemical peel, in which, for about two hundred dollars a treatment, the top layer of skin is burned away with salicylic acid, taking surface wrinkles with it. In fact, the chemical peel has become so fast and painless that I wouldn't be surprised to see it done soon as a spray that you can keep on your bathroom sink, right beside your deodorant. First you perfume your underarms, and then you erase your face.

There also is collagen, which has become the hot new semi–face-lift. No, not lifting half your face: instead, lifting all your face about half the degree of cosmetic surgery. The standard injections of collagen (usually from cowhide) fill in the wrinkles that have made your face look like the roads into O'Hare. At a cost of about four hundred dollars, a collagen shot lasts about six months before it dissolves. That comes to roughly two dollars a day to repave your face.

And last year came the first *non*standard injection of collagen when a woman who had just given birth was injected with the collagen from her baby's umbilical cord to puff up her lips and erase her few small facial lines. Such postpartum elation may become standard procedure.

"It gave me the gift of youth," said that mother.

And I had thought the gift of youth was that small bundle they put in the crib. At least she didn't try to smooth out any wrinkles on the baby.

Recently, an injection of vitamins was developed that stimulates your body to produce more of its natural collagen. At a cost of about four hundred dollars, you can rejuvenate your face with two or three shots.

A remarkable new antiwrinkle treatment called yeast cell therapy smooths out the skin by delivering oxygen directly to the collagen you already have. It is now easy to have your face ironed.

Now let's leave the face and join all those people, men as well as women, who see their bodies as fleshy Erector sets that can be reconstructed. Last night, I heard a woman in her early forties say, "For my next birthday, I'm having my veins done."

She could have been talking about getting her varicose veins untangled and moved to a more pleasing depth; or she could have been talking about spider veins. I recently had the spider veins on my feet removed. For whom did I do it? For me. Now gone at last are those multicolored arachnids that were all but crawling under my skin and depressed me whenever I had to look down on them.

And now we come to those thunder thighs. No, don't stand in front of your mirror and weep: Have them liposuctioned down to human size, and your baggy buttocks too. While in the neighborhood, let's round the corner and erase those stretch marks with a tummy tuck.

We have finally reached your breasts. Or, if you're like me, we have passed them on our trip north. Are yours fat and pendulous, always getting underfoot? Then hew them down and perk them up with a surgical reduction-cum-lift. Or, if they're too flat, consider saline or peanut oil implants. They're squishier than silicone, but 100 percent safe.

Unfortunately, there is nothing surgical you can do about wrinkled or crepey hands. However, a dermatologist *can* burn off age spots. Or you can ask your doctor to give you a prescription for Renova, a cream containing Retin-A, that can bleach brown spots and prevent further wrinkling and dryness.

There is also a lot you can do to save your own skin without the aid of a doctor. According to Dr. Wilma F. Bergfeld, head of clinical research in the department of dermatology at the Cleveland Clinic Foundation, a woman can actually rejuvenate herself from head to toe.

First—and do this at about thirty-five—say goodbye to the sun. I happened to bid the sun adieu much earlier, when I was in college. I remember saying to my roommate, "I'm not going out there in direct sunlight. I've got enough to contend with without crow's-feet." It was one of the smartest decisions of my life.

Even after you've dropped your friendship with the sun, you shouldn't go outdoors on a summer day without a sunscreen of at least SPF 15. If you think SPF 15 is a motor oil, then no matter how hard you try to shade your skin, it's headed for the compost heap.

Dr. Bergfeld says that, in addition to wearing SPF 15, you should also wear a hat that shades you from the sun and a shirt that covers your chest. Her advice is easy for me to follow: I have never minded wearing anything that prevents a sobering view of my chest.

My elbows have never been intoxicating and I suspect that neither are yours; all that leaning and chafing makes the skin look tough and scaly. However, Dr. Bergfeld has a suggestion for keeping your elbows from looking as though they belong on an elephant: Soften the skin by gently scrubbing your elbows with a loofah sponge every time you bathe.

Your feet also need special attention, for their skin becomes dry, thin, and wrinkled through the years. The doctor suggests that you drench them with moisturizers containing alpha-hydroxy acids, which will slough off dead skin to reveal a fresh new layer. Show the world your hidden depths.

Clearly, cosmetic surgery is the best way to rejuvenate yourself, but between those biannual tune-ups, you should spend a few days at a spa. What could make you feel more sybaritic than a concentrated period of good food, invigorating exercise, soothing massage, luxurious body wraps, revitalizing facials, and a total makeover stopping just short of cut and paste?

"I'd need a second mortgage to afford that kind of spa," you're saying, and I understand: A trip to a spa isn't a trip to the zoo. However, you can create your *own* spa of sorts by treating yourself to a masseuse now and then and topping off your workouts with a long hot bath. Given your otherwise disciplined life, you deserve to pamper yourself a bit.

I'm allowed to pamper myself because I'm disciplined too, although I did embroider these words on a pillow in my den:

LIFE IS UNCERTAIN
EAT DESSERT FIRST

In creating your own little spa, nothing beats the luxury of a bath, which is better for your morale than a shower. Cleopatra never jumped into a shower.

Why is a bath better than a shower?

1. The reclining position is less stressful to your body than standing.

2. The muscles in your feet, legs, and back are at rest.

3. Your breathing comes more easily.

4. The heat is more uniform.

5. The heated water covers a greater area of your body, causing all your blood vessels to dilate so that you feel really relaxed.

6. You can scent the water with fragrant bath salts and bubble bath. Try *that* in a shower.

7. You can pour in aromatic moisturizers made especially for the tub, and your body is in constant contact with them.

In a bath, the combination of the water caressing your body, the steam, and the long-lasting fragrance makes the soaking an intense and voluptuous experience. You can burn incense, light candles, and sip champagne. You might even share it all with a friend.

Why It's Great to Be Twenty

- Your entire life lies ahead, unless you're living in a trailer and already have six children.

- You have finally realized that Leonardo DiCaprio is a complete idiot.

- You do not remember how truly annoying the Beatles were when they were all together.

- You need only one cake for all your birthday candles.

Why It's Great to Be Thirty

- Men will still open doors for you, especially ones leading to their bedrooms.

- Men still find you alluring, at least when there's no woman around in her twenties.

- You are learning to pick your men for something deeper and more significant than looks: money.

- You finally know better than to accept a car ride with a Kennedy.

- Nobody laughed you out of the room when you auditioned for Baywatch.

Why It's Great to Be Forty

- You're not fifty yet.

- You now judge men the same way you expect to be judged: by their bodies.

- Your night table is only half filled with medications.

- You find yourself agreeing completely with your mother.

Why It's Great to Be Fifty

- You now know the most important thing in choosing a man: by whether his divorce is final.

- The highlight of your day is not yet a mail delivery.

- You understand Picasso, but weren't there when he went through his blue period.

- You use Polygrip only for sealing your windows in the winter.

- You still get hit on by men who date Anna Nicole Smith.

Why It's Great to Be Sixty

- Your doctor has not yet begun to use the phrase, "You again?"

- You can visit a castle without remembering what it was like before it went up.

- You no longer have to close your drapes because nobody is going to look in anyway.

- Corn on the cob won't make you fat because it's no longer an option.

Why It's Great to Be Seventy

- You can ask younger people to do things for you, like carry your packages or clean your dentures.

- When you get on a bus, even the driver will offer you a seat.

- The insurance for the car that your children no longer allow you to drive has finally dropped to a decent rate.

Why It's Great to Be Eighty

- You can refer to John Glenn as a "whippersnapper."

- You realize the importance of the time you have left and watch every VCR tape on fast forward.

- You can finally admit you bought an Edsel.

- You now have learned to say "I don't remember" in six languages.

- You can admit that what first caused you to live in New York was the Indians.

Why It's Great to Be Ninety

- You won't get fat because solid food is no longer an option.

- Your body has sagged so much your tattoos are no longer readable.

- You can follow the noun "sex" with the verb "was" without being embarrassed.

- You can dress as hip as you want: with your cap backward and baggy pants and underwear hanging out of the top, for most older people do this naturally.

Why It's Great to Be One Hundred

- All your enemies are dead.

- You have to have *two* birthday cakes to make room for all your candles.

- Movies let you in free out of sympathy.

- Your children no longer annoy you because you can no longer hear or see them.

TEN

The Luckier You Get

Nobody likes aging.

Not Doris Day, who once said, "The really frightening thing about middle age is that you know you'll grow out of it."

Not Tom Stoppard, who once said, "Age is a high price to pay for maturity."

Not Lady Nancy Astor, British MP, who once said, "I refuse to admit that I'm more than fifty-two, even if that does make my sons illegitimate."

And not Joan Rivers, who tells people, "I was born in 1962. And the room next to mine was 1963."

If aging were only a joke! But it's not and we cannot laugh it off. There is nothing funny about aging: It is rotten and depressing. Anyone who tells you otherwise just hasn't been paying attention. All those magazines that trumpet the pleasures of aging are lying to us. Willard Scott is lying to us on the *Today Show* when he celebrates Aunt Bessie's one hundredth birthday and tells us what a wonderful time she is having in her walker. Please don't insult our intelligence, Willard. No one who is sitting in damp Depends wants to be told that this is a wonderful moment in her life. She has probably been looking for Dr. Kevorkian's number.

If I had a license to kill everyone who lied to me about the glories of aging, there'd be a bloodbath.

My own mother happened to be the first person who ever told me the truth about aging.

"Joan," she said, "getting older is horrific, but you have to go through it. And not just through it, but through it with dignity."

And that's precisely what I have been trying to do ever since: Go through it with dignity. It hasn't been easy—in fact, at times it's been brutally hard—but doing the very hard, sometimes the seemingly impossible, has become a part of most women's lives. I am a woman who bounced back after losing her husband, her TV show, her Broadway show, her jewelry business, her credit rating, her daughter's best wishes, and her reason to get up in the morning—or the early afternoon. I am a woman who, at one point a few years ago, was flat on her back—and not for the best reason to assume that position.

However, from these multifaceted depths, I managed to bounce back, and after a brief period of feeling sorry for myself, I regained a rapport with my daughter, fought my way out of bankruptcy, began writing a new play, and gave rebirth to a career for which people were lighting candles.

Although I am now riding an incredibly happy wave in my life, I still don't want to be one day older. However, since I also don't want to be stupid, I now realize the profound wisdom of this thought: "The older I get, the luckier I am." There is simply no other way to look at aging!

Sure, I've been through a generous portion of hell, but I certainly can't change one bit of it. The only person who can change the past is a sloppy historian, so I concentrate on changing the present. A person with even a modest IQ knows that the present is the only place to live—except for South Hampton, of course. And so I spend all my time living in the *now,* not in the *way back when* or the *one day when.*

If you're smart, you'll approach aging with both mellowness and grit, with both serenity and an iron will, with both peace and passionate discipline. Aging still will suck, but it needn't entirely suck you in. If you are smart, you will resist aging sensibly: not by mindlessly worshiping youth but by making your life as good as it can be at *every* age—except sixteen. At sixteen, the only help you need is Dermasil.

"Yes, I've been trying to hold on to every element of my youth," says Faye Wattleton, head of the Center for Gender Equality. "I don't think there's anything wrong with that. If we can retard the process of aging, the quality of life is improved because aging does bring certain changes."

Absolutely, Faye. One of the changes it brings is a clicking in our joints when we get out of bed that leaves us wanting to be greased and lubed. But if you stagger to the mirror and from time to time, with almost total honesty, you can say: "I'm amazing for my age. I *look* amazing, *feel* amazing, and my *life* is amazing too," then you are winning the silent battle we all are fighting and you will have done it all by yourself!

You've got to realize that life is not a tennis match: There are no rules. You don't need to go to Tibet to learn that, for common sense tells us that life is a matter of choices, and you have to base yours on what feels right for you at any given moment. If you're smart, you will *seize* every moment. I don't want to hear you say, "Why go to Europe since I only have four days?" Take five days. Europe is small, days are long, you'll regret not having gone.

I went to St. Petersburg—no, not the one in Florida—for three days in the middle of the winter. All my friends said, "Three days? What can you do in three days? Wait till you have at least a week." Well, it was the best trip of my life. I stood in the Hermitage and I walked the streets that Peter the Great walked and I had thirty-two kinds of borscht and I saw a performance of the opera *Navista*. Three magical, unforgettable days.

Kim Basinger once said, "When I'm old, I'm never going to say, 'I didn't do this' or 'I regret that,' I'm going to say, 'I don't regret a damn thing. I came, I went, and I did it all.'"

If you are smart and eat right and exercise well and have been suctioned out and can suck in your gut and hold it, if you've taken that long hard look in the mirror and decided you still look great at fifty, then you will put on that bandage dress by Leger and flaunt it and know that people will think you look terrific and the hell with your age!

If you are smart, you will also accept reality. If the hard look in the mirror tells you that you can't wear that Leger, then know that at least you can still look up-to-date and not like someone who was just pulled off the *Titanic*.

"That's easy for you to say, Joan," you're telling me. "You can afford gyms and spas and vacations and new clothes."

However, money *isn't* the key to staying youthful and attractive. As I have said, the best exercise is *free* and the best grooming is simple and cheap. Brushing your hair, using makeup intelligently, and wearing a nice piece of jewelry with simple, tailored clothes does not require a sale of stock.

And, if you are smart, you'll understand that, every once in a while, you're going to slip up and look like a fool, so keep your sense of humor and remember you can always regroup. I used to love to dance at discos, to make up my own steps and be carefree on the floor, but there comes a moment when you realize that this particular woman should no longer be hopping around under the spinning mirror ball.

Mine came several years ago in Greece. I was on vacation with Melissa, a man, and his two daughters. We all decided to go dancing and headed for a trendy new disco. When the girls got up on the floor, the man and I joined them. Suddenly I noticed that we were the only people over forty who were dancing, and when the lights hit him, he looked like an elderly, portly fool, and I knew I looked equally alluring—even more so next to all those long-legged, suntanned, hormone-happy Greek girls. At once I pulled him off the floor and we became spectators for the rest of the night.

That was a very hard moment for me, but you simply have to learn when it's time to sit out the dance.

And, if you're smart, you will heed this list of seven essentials you need as the years creep up, essentials set down by Dr. Richard Restak in *Older and Wiser:*

- Curiosity.

- Keeping busy.

- Regular exercise and physical activity.

- Acceptance of unavoidable limitations.

- Need for diversity and novelty.

- Maintenance of friends and social networks.

- Links with younger people.

If you are smart, you will also know that you've got to have hope. My friend Tyne Daly says, "Hope is a muscle." In other words, you have to keep exercising it. Emily Dickinson wrote, "Hope is a thing with feathers," but I prefer Tyne's definition. Anyway, Emily Dickinson never got out of the house, so what did *she* know? I want *you* to get out of the house, and I want you to believe what I do: that good things even come out of bad ones. In fact, I've rarely seen anything bad that didn't lead to something positive.

But you've got to keep making the positive happen; you've got to work at turning around whatever befalls you so that it works to your advantage. For example, if you have a hysterectomy, make them give you a tummy tuck at the same time. Somebody has to sew you up, so let it be a plastic surgeon. That's what *I* did, and I was the only happy lady on my floor. The other women were moaning, "Oh, it's over; what's left for me?" But *I* was looking down at my stomach and thinking: *I can wear a two-piece bathing suit again!*

Try to turn everything to your advantage. If your feet hurt and you can't take another step in heels, say, "Aren't I lucky that this year flats are in." And you're wearing them not because your feet hurt but because you're hip.

In the words of the song: Accentuate the positive and eliminate the negative. Not only should you not dwell on the negative, but avoid friends who dwell on it. Whenever you're forced to talk to such a friend, simply tune her out, remain upbeat, and get away fast.

"How are you?" you'll say to the negative one.

"Life stinks," she'll reply. "I'm burned out, bewitched, bothered, and bewildered."

"Right. And the kids?"

"The older one ran away last week. The younger one goes to trial on Monday. I'm really upset: I have nothing to wear."

"What a pity; got to go. Have a good day."

People who tell me they feel burned out drive me up the wall (which at least is good exercise), because it really means they are bored, and there's no excuse for being bored, unless you happen to be in solitary confinement. It is the height—well, really the depth—of stupidity to feel burned out on a planet overflowing with the riches that Robert Louis Stevenson recommended to children with the words:

The world is so full of a number of things,
I'm sure we should all be as happy as kings.

All right, it's hard to find a king happy today, except maybe Larry, but we're living in a world that Stevenson never dreamed of, and it is inexcusably dumb to say you are bored or burned out or bummed out or anything but overwhelmed by the possibilities and the delights. Forget the Sears catalog and read the one from your local community college and your YWCA. Volunteer to play with children in hospitals or work at an Adult Literacy Center and see how quickly your burnout is extinguished.

The Beatles may have believed in yesterdays when they sang as a group, but Paul McCartney offstage has always believed in today. Right after the tragic death of his wife, Linda, he spoke of the philosophy that had kept the two of them happy for thirty years.

"If I could have just one wish, it would be to enjoy today. That's it. If I can go to bed at night and say, 'Yeah, that was good,' then that really is all there is."

Yesterday is a ghost and tomorrow is a dream. It is always *right now*. Be thankful that God has given you this right now. Many of your friends and loved ones no longer have it, so *enjoy it*. You don't have to be Einstein to figure that out. The Three Stooges knew it. They laughed till they dropped.

Why You Should Be Happy at the Age You Are Right Now

- Because for fifty years you never had to go through the trauma of dealing with an HMO.

- Because, at your age, you grew up not knowing there were two meanings to the slogan, "All the way with JFK."

- Because you learned the facts of life where they should be learned: at drive-in movies.

- Because you never had a job as a Clinton intern.

- Because you know your money isn't in rubles.

- Because you always knew that everyone on *Father Knows Best* was a total idiot.

- Because an earthquake never happened when you were in the shower.

- Because you can remember when Elvis was thin and still in the building.

- Because at your age, you have enough money to buy this book, eyesight good enough to read it, and brain power skilled enough to understand it— Isn't life grand! ☺